ELEMENTARY
Student's Book

in English

PETER VINEY
KAREN VINEY

OXFORD
UNIVERSITY PRESS

OXFORD
UNIVERSITY PRESS

Great Clarendon Street, Oxford OX2 6DP

Oxford University Press is a department of the University of Oxford.
It furthers the University's objective of excellence in research, scholarship,
and education by publishing worldwide in

Oxford New York

Auckland Cape Town Dar es Salaam Hong Kong Karachi
Kuala Lumpur Madrid Melbourne Mexico City Nairobi
New Delhi Shanghai Taipei Toronto

With offices in

Argentina Austria Brazil Chile Czech Republic France Greece
Guatemala Hungary Italy Japan Poland Portugal Singapore
South Korea Switzerland Thailand Turkey Ukraine Vietnam

OXFORD and OXFORD ENGLISH are registered trade marks of
Oxford University Press in the UK and in certain other countries

© Oxford University Press / Three Vee Limited 2004

The moral rights of the author have been asserted

Database right Oxford University Press (maker)

First published 2004
2014 2013 2012 2011
10 9

No unauthorized photocopying

All rights reserved. No part of this publication may be reproduced,
stored in a retrieval system, or transmitted, in any form or by any means,
without the prior permission in writing of Oxford University Press,
or as expressly permitted by law, or under terms agreed with the
appropriate reprographics rights organization. Enquiries concerning
reproduction outside the scope of the above should be sent to the
ELT Rights Department, Oxford University Press, at the address above

You must not circulate this book in any other binding or cover
and you must impose this same condition on any acquirer

Any websites referred to in this publication are in the public
domain and their addresses are provided by Oxford University Press
for information only. Oxford University Press disclaims any
responsibility for the content

ISBN: 978 0 19 434056 4

Typeset in Meta

Printed in China

ACKNOWLEDGEMENT
Designed by Richard Morris, Stonesfield Design

Contents

	UNIT TITLE	GRAMMAR	TOPICS
1	Meeting people	*be*: singular Subject pronouns: singular Possessive adjectives: singular	Introductions Names Numbers 0-10
2	Greetings	*be*: plural Subject pronouns: plural Possessive adjectives: plural	Greetings Numbers 11-20 Personal questions
3	Food and drink	Minimal language for requests Indefinite articles: *a / an* Questions	Requests Food and drink Prices
4	Talking about things	*be*: It's (a) ... / They're ... Demonstratives: adjectives Singular and plural: *a, an, the*	Large numbers Colours
5	Have you got ...?	*have*: have got / has got Countables: *some / any* What...? Who ...? What (kind) ...?	Appointments Suggestions Days of the week
6	Work	Present simple: all persons	Routines Work Jobs
7	Home	Present simple Quantity: *How many?* Adjectives	Describing places Addresses, e-mail Facilities
8	Travel	Time Present simple	Information Travel Transport
9	Instructions	Imperative / base forms Object pronouns Prepositions of place	Instructions Warnings Location
10	Can and can't	*can / can't* Ability Permission	Food Lexical verbs

CONTENTS

	UNIT TITLE	GRAMMAR	TOPICS
11	Is there any water?	Countables and uncountables Possessive 's with nouns	Quantity Food
12	What would you like?	I'd like / would like Questions – *any* Offers – *some*	Requests Offers Shopping
13	Shopping in London	Prepositions Present continuous formulas *can*	Directions Ordinals (1) Film, music
14	What are you doing?	Present continuous: *doing / happening*	Actions Families Mealtimes
15	I like it	Likes and dislikes *-ing* forms: *so, really* *I like / I'd like*	Compliments Pastimes Hobbies
16	Talking about the future	Present continuous future *going to* for predictions and intentions Future time words	Arrangements Weather Months Ordinals (2)
17	was and were	Past: *was / were* *be born* Past time words	Dates Ordinals (3) Facts
18	What did you do?	Past simple: irregular verbs High-frequency irregular verbs Question words	Holidays Breakfast
19	What happened?	Past simple: regular verbs *born, engaged, married, divorced, died*	Personal details Biographies Life events
20	True stories	Past simple: regular, irregular Subject / object questions Introductory adverbs	Narrative Movement Story techniques

CONTENTS

	UNIT TITLE	GRAMMAR	TOPICS
21	Healthy living	Frequency adverbs: *How often?* *once / twice / 3 times a (week)* *good for you / bad for you*	Habits Routines Diet, exercise
22	His clothes, her clothes	Present simple and present continuous Adjectives	Describing people Clothes Appearance
23	Have you ever ...?	Present perfect: *been, seen* *Have you ever ...? ... yet* Contrast past simple, *going to*	Experiences Places Travel
24	What have you done?	Present perfect with irregular verbs + regular verbs Present time words	Life experience Daily experience Sport
25	I'll do it ...	*will*: functional uses Requests, deciding, agreeing promising, refusing, apologizing	Family life
26	Predictions	*will + be, will + do:* future uses *It depends ... / plenty of ...*	Prediction Travel
27	Comparisons	Comparatives Superlatives	The future Books, films records
28	Best friend	Narrative in the past simple Frequency adverbs Adverbs of manner	Habits
29	I've got to stay in	*have to / have got to, had to, could, couldn't* Reasons: *because*	Invitations Obligation
30	Want to do	Infinitive patterns Reasons: *so, because* Infinitive of purpose	Hopes, fears Ambitions Shops

Know your book

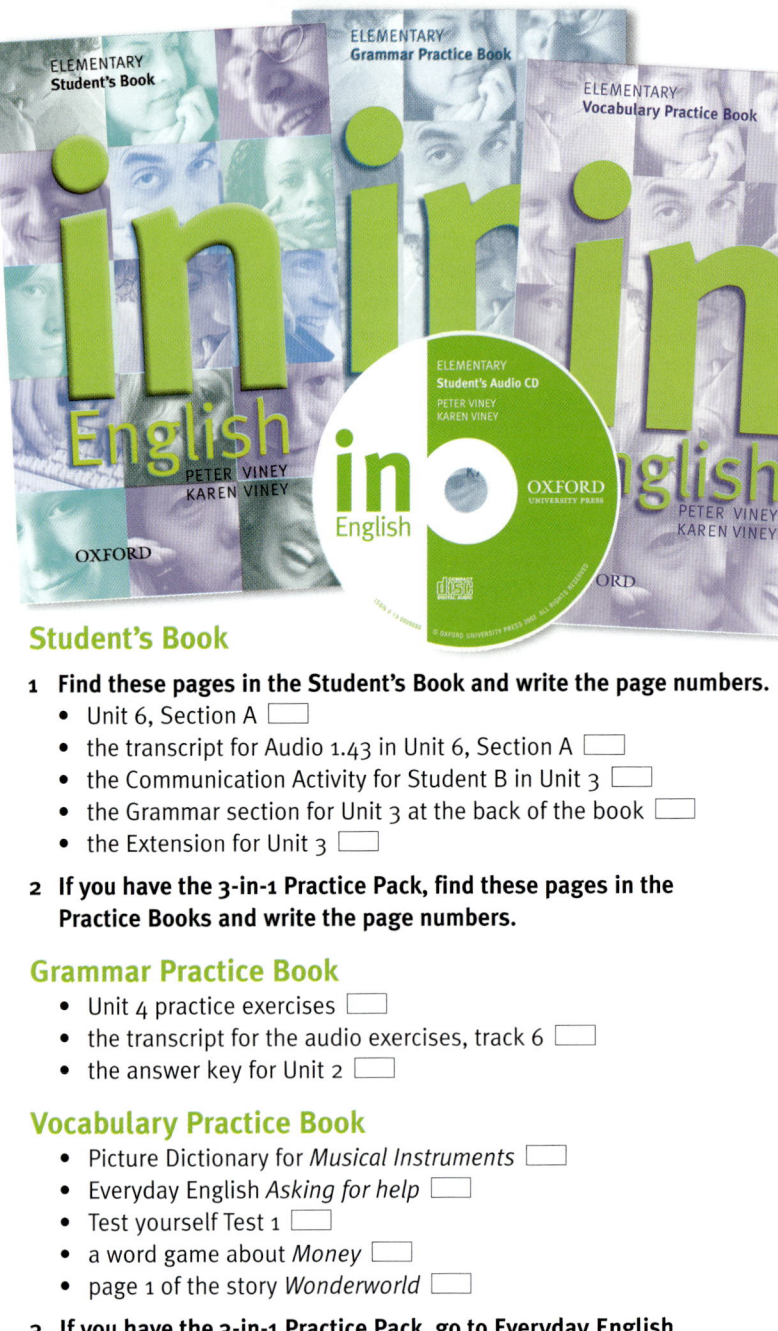

Student's Book

1 **Find these pages in the Student's Book and write the page numbers.**
   - Unit 6, Section A ☐
   - the transcript for Audio 1.43 in Unit 6, Section A ☐
   - the Communication Activity for Student B in Unit 3 ☐
   - the Grammar section for Unit 3 at the back of the book ☐
   - the Extension for Unit 3 ☐

2 **If you have the 3-in-1 Practice Pack, find these pages in the Practice Books and write the page numbers.**

Grammar Practice Book
   - Unit 4 practice exercises ☐
   - the transcript for the audio exercises, track 6 ☐
   - the answer key for Unit 2 ☐

Vocabulary Practice Book
   - Picture Dictionary for *Musical Instruments* ☐
   - Everyday English *Asking for help* ☐
   - Test yourself Test 1 ☐
   - a word game about *Money* ☐
   - page 1 of the story *Wonderworld* ☐

3 **If you have the 3-in-1 Practice Pack, go to Everyday English** *Asking for help* **and practise the expressions.**

Classroom language

Do you understand the instructions? Write a translation.

Look.

Listen.

Say.

Repeat.

Ask.

Answer.

Read.

Write.

Think.

Open / Close the book.

Pair work.

Group work.

Match.

Underline.

Tick / Choose the correct word.

Maria *is* from Spain.

Complete the sentences.

Circle the correct word.

Highlight the correct word.

1 Meeting people

A Hello ...

1 Listen. 1.02
- Hello.
- Hello.
- My name's Kylie. What's your name?
- Josh.
- Good to meet you, Josh.
- Good to meet you, too.

Good	to meet you.
Pleased	
Nice	
Great	

2 Pair work. Ask and answer.
- Hi, my name's ....
What's your name?
- Hi, ...
My name's ....
- .... to meet you,
....
- .... to meet you, too.

B Where are you from?

1 Match Josh's questions and Kylie's answers.

Question
1 Are you the teacher?
2 Are you English?
3 Really? Where are you from?

Answer
A No, I'm not. I'm Australian.
B I'm from Sydney.
C Yes, I am.

Listen and check. ✱ 1.03

2 Pair work. Ask and answer.
▶ Are you English?
◀ No, I'm not. I'm ....
▶ Where are you from?
◀ I'm from ....

---

be: singular
I'm English.   **You're** a student.
He's from France.   **She's** Australian.
I'm not English.   **She isn't** a teacher.   **You aren't** from London.

Are you English?   Yes, **I am**. / No, **I'm not**.
Is he American?   Yes, **he is**. / No, **he isn't**.
Where **are you** from?
Where**'s she** from?

Possessive adjectives
My name**'s** Josh.   **His** name**'s** Sam.
Your name**'s** Anna.   **Her** name**'s** Maria.

---

3 Write the contractions.
is not = isn't
1 I am = ...
2 He is = ...
3 She is = ...
4 You are = ...
5 What is = ...
6 are not = ...

	A	B	C	D
Name	Sam	Sarah	Fiona	Patrick
Country	The USA	Canada	Scotland	Ireland
Nationality	American	Canadian	Scottish	Irish

4 Ask and answer about the people. ✱ 1.04

Picture A
- ▶ What's his name?
- ◀ His name's Sam.
- ▶ Is he English?
- ◀ No, he isn't. He's American.
- ▶ Where's he from?
- ◀ He's from the USA.

C Spelling

1 The alphabet.
Listen and repeat. ✱ 1.05

/iː/	B C D E G P T V
/e/	F L M N S X Z
/eɪ/	A H J K
/uː/	Q U W
/aɪ/	I Y
/əʊ/	O
/ɑː/	R

Harley Sports Centre
FITNESS CLASS REGISTER
Teacher: Ms Kylie Winton

Title	First name	Family name	Phone number
Mr	Josh		
Mr	Sam		
Mrs	Sarah		
Miss	Fiona		
Mr	Patrick		

Say aloud.
USA BBC IBM EU MTV CNN OUP DVD AEI

T = capital t   t = small t   tt = double t
Can you spell that? Can you repeat that?

2 Listen and write the family names on the register. ✱ 1.06 – 1.10

3 Pair work. Ask and answer.
- ▶ What's your name?
- ◀ My name's ....
- ▶ Can you spell that?
- ◀ Yes. ....

D What's your phone number?

1 Numbers. Listen and repeat. ✱ 1.11
zero or 'O'   one   two   three   four   five
six   seven   eight   nine   ten
double six   double 'O'

2 Listen and write the phone numbers on the register. ✱ 1.12

3 Pair work. Ask and answer.
- ▶ What's your phone number?
- ◀ My number's ....

E See you ...

1 Listen. ✱ 1.13
- ■ Goodbye, Patrick.
- ● 'Bye, Fiona.
- ■ See you next lesson.
- ● Yes, see you.

2 Which words can you add to *See you ...*? Tick (✓) the boxes.
- ☐ later
- ☐ again
- ☐ soon
- ☐ yesterday
- ☐ next lesson

Can you think of more words to add to *See you ...*?
Say *Goodbye* / *See you ...* to students in your class.

See **Extension 1** p.160

2 Greetings

A How are you?

1 Listen. Practise the conversations.

✱ 1.14

Jenny Good morning, Mr Hope.
Mr Hope Good morning, Jenny. How are you?
Jenny I'm very well, thank you. And you?
Mr Hope I'm fine, thanks.

✱ 1.15

Kevin Hi.
Jenny Hi. I'm late for work. See you tonight!
Kevin Yeah, see you. 'Bye!

✱ 1.18

Kevin Hi, Jenny.
Jenny Hi, Kevin. This is my mother. Mum, this is Kevin.
Kevin Good evening, Mrs Ashton.
Mrs A. Good evening, Kevin.

(✳ 1.16)
Wendy Hello, Jenny.
Jenny Hello, Wendy. Sorry I'm late.

(✳ 1.17)
Jenny Good afternoon, sir, madam.
Man Good afternoon.
A table for two, please.
Jenny Yes, sir. Over there …

(✳ 1.19)
Kevin Goodnight, Jenny.
Jenny Goodnight, Kevin. Thanks for a lovely evening.

2 **Formal or informal?**
Put *F* (formal) or *I* (informal) with these words.
☐ Good morning. ☐ Hi.
☐ See you. ☐ Hello.
☐ Good evening. ☐ 'Bye.
☐ Jenny ☐ Mr Hope
☐ madam ☐ sir
☐ Mrs Ashton ☐ Kevin
☐ Good afternoon.

3 **Introduce students in your class.**
▶ Anna. This is Paul. Paul, this is Anna.
◀ Nice to meet you, Paul.
▶ Nice to meet you, Anna.

B Check-in

1 Listen. ✱ 1.20
Tourist Good evening.
A family room, please.
Receptionist Nice accent!
Are you British?
Tourist Yes, we are.
Receptionist Where are you from?
Tourist We're from Dover.
Receptionist Oh, really? How old
are your children?
Tourist Sorry?
Receptionist Are they under
fourteen?
Tourist Yes, they are. She's twelve
and he's eleven.
Receptionist Right. Kids stay free.

2 Ask and answer.
1 Are the tourists British or American?
2 Where are they from?
3 Are their children over fourteen, or under fourteen?
4 How old are they?

Kids under-14 *stay free*

---

be: plural
We're tourists. **You're** students. **They aren't** here.
Are you tourists? Yes, **we are**. / No, **we aren't**.

Possessive adjectives: plural
Their children are under fourteen. **Our** class is in room five.
Dan and Anna, **your** books are here.

3 Choose the correct words.
1 (They're / Their) students.
2 (They're / Their) class is in room five.
3 (We're / Our) teacher isn't British.
4 (We're / Our) in class now.
5 Paul and Maria, (your / you) aren't listening.
6 Hello, Sarah! How are (your / you're) children?
7 Are you students? Yes, (we're / we are).

C Numbers 11 to 99

1 Listen and repeat the numbers. (✱ 1.21)

11 eleven	20 twenty	21 twenty-one
12 twelve	30 thirty	38 thirty-eight
13 thirteen	40 forty	45 forty-five
14 fourteen	50 fifty	52 fifty-two
15 fifteen	60 sixty	64 sixty-four
16 sixteen	70 seventy	73 seventy-three
17 seventeen	80 eighty	89 eighty-nine
18 eighteen	90 ninety	97 ninety-seven
19 nineteen		

RU 18

★ LIVE UNDER-21 EUROPEAN ★
CHAMPIONSHIP FOOTBALL, 7.15PM
How will our boys fare against Italy?

CLUB 18-30

50% discount for over-65s

CAR RENTALS over 25s ONLY

2 Listen and write the numbers in the spaces. (✱ 1.22)

ACME MAIL ORDER — Telephone order

- Name: Peter Smith
- Credit card number: ☐☐☐☐ / ☐☐☐☐ / ☐☐☐☐ / ☐☐☐☐
- Expiry date: ☐☐ / ☐☐
- Date of birth: ☐☐ / ☐☐ / ☐☐
- Address: Flat ☐☐ , ☐☐ West Street, Camford
- Postcode: ☐☐☐☐ ☐☐☐
- Telephone number: _____
- Order reference: ☐☐ / ☐☐ / ☐☐ / ☐☐ / ☐☐ / ☐☐

3 Ask and answer about the people in the picture.

▶ How old is the mother?
◀ I don't know. / She's about forty.

D Personal questions

1 ~~Cross out~~ **the questions that are not polite in your country.**

1. How old are you?
2. What's your date of birth?
3. Are you married or single?
4. Why aren't you married?
5. Are you rich?
6. How are you?
7. How are your parents?
8. How are your children?
9. What's your address?
10. What nationality are you?
11. What blood group are you?
12. What religion are you?
13. What's your phone number?
14. Where are you from?

If you don't want to answer …

I don't want to answer that.

Sorry, that's a personal question.

Mind your own business!

2 Ask your partner the questions in 1.

See **Extension 2** p.161

3 Food and drink

A International words

1. International words are the same, or nearly the same, in different languages.
   Group work. Make three lists. Add more international words.
2. Compare your lists with another group.

Places to eat and drink	Things to eat	Things to drink
pizzeria	sandwich	espresso
bar	croissant	champagne

B Coffee shop

MENU

DRINKS
filter coffee	black / white	1.50
espresso	single	1.40
	double	1.90
cappuccino		2.10
iced coffee		1.80
tea	cup	1.30
	pot for one	1.80
	pot for two	3.60
hot chocolate		1.70
mineral water	still / sparkling	1.20
soft drinks	regular	1.30
cola / lemonade	large	2.00
fruit juice	apple / orange	1.90

FOOD
Danish pastry	chocolate / almond	1.95
Croissant	with butter and jam	2.15
American muffin	chocolate / blueberry	1.75
Chocolate donut		1.50
Slice of pizza		2.65
Sandwiches	tuna / egg and bacon	3.00
Baguettes	egg / cheese and tomato	3.99

A ....
B ....
C ....
D ....
E ....
F ....

1 **What is it? Write the words from the menu.**

2 **How much is it? Look at the menu and write the prices. Listen and check.** ✱1.23

3 **Listen and repeat.** ✱1.24
Black or white?   Single or double?   Still or sparkling?
Regular or large?   Apple or orange?   Chocolate or almond?
Chocolate or blueberry?

4 **Listen and repeat.** ✱1.25
and   'n'
butter 'n' jam   egg 'n' bacon   cheese 'n' tomato

Use **a** before the sound of a consonant:
b, c, d, f, g, h, j, k, l, m, n, p, q, r, s, t, v, w, x, y, z

Use **an** before the sound of a vowel: a, e, i, o, u

5 Put *a* or *an* before these words.

.... baguette .... espresso .... apple juice
.... egg sandwich .... pot of tea .... mineral water
.... tuna sandwich .... orange juice

C Conversations

1 Listen. Practise the conversation. (✲ 1.26)

Customer An espresso and a pot of tea for one, please.
Server Single or double espresso?
Customer Single.
Server Anything to eat?
Customer No, thanks.
How much is that?
Server Three twenty.

2 Complete the conversation with these sentences.

Anything else?   That's six fifty.   Regular or large?
You're welcome.   Anything to drink?   Can I help you?

Server ....
Customer Yes, an egg and bacon sandwich, please.
Server ....
Customer Yes, a chocolate doughnut.
Server ....
Customer Yes, please. A lemonade.
Server ....
Customer Large.
Server ....
Customer Thank you.
Server ....

3 Listen and check. (✲ 1.27)
Practise the conversation.

4 Pair work. Make conversations using the menu.

D Listening

1 **Listen.** (✱ 1.28)
Who says these things? Write *F* (the father), *D* (the daughter), or *S* (the son).
1 Let's have something to eat.
2 Are you hungry?
3 Pizza for me.
4 How about a sandwich?
5 It's my favourite.
6 And for you, Victoria?
7 I'm on a diet!
8 I'm vegetarian!
9 How about a cheese and tomato sandwich?
10 No, thanks. Just an orange juice.

Listen again and check.

2 **Listen. Tick (✓) the things that the father orders. How much is it altogether?** (✱ 1.29)
  ☐ a slice of pizza
  ☐ a chocolate doughnut
  ☐ a cheese and tomato sandwich
  ☐ an orange juice
  ☐ a pot of tea
  ☐ an egg and bacon sandwich
  ☐ an almond Danish pastry
  ☐ a cola
  ☐ a cup of tea
  ☐ a lemonade

COMMUNICATION

Student A Look at Activity 1 on p.190.
Student B Look at Activity 13 on p.199.

See **Extension 3** p.162

4 Talking about things

A Describing paintings

1 **Underline the sentences about the Mona Lisa. Tick (✓) the sentences about the cave paintings.**
These are cave paintings.
Her smile is famous.
It's by Leonardo da Vinci.
They're in caves in Chauvet, France.
It's about five hundred years old.
They're thirty thousand years old.
The caves are closed. You can't see the paintings.
This is the Mona Lisa.
They are pictures of rhinos.
They're by prehistoric artists.
It's in the Louvre in Paris.
Thousands of people see the painting every day.

Listen and check. ✱ 1.30

2 **Ask and answer.**
Who is it by?   Who are they by?
Where is it?   Where are they?
How old is it?   How old are they?
What's famous about it? What are they pictures of?

3 **Listen to the tour guide.** ✱ 1.31
Correct the wrong information.

B What is it? / What are they?

1 Find these things in the pictures.

> apple bed bird bowl cat chair coat jug orange
> plate ship star station table train tree umbrella
> watch window

2 Change the singular words in 1 to plural words.

3 Ask and answer about the pictures.
- ▶ What is it?
- ◀ It's (*a ship / a watch / an orange*).
- ▶ What are they?
- ◀ They're (*ships / watches / oranges*).

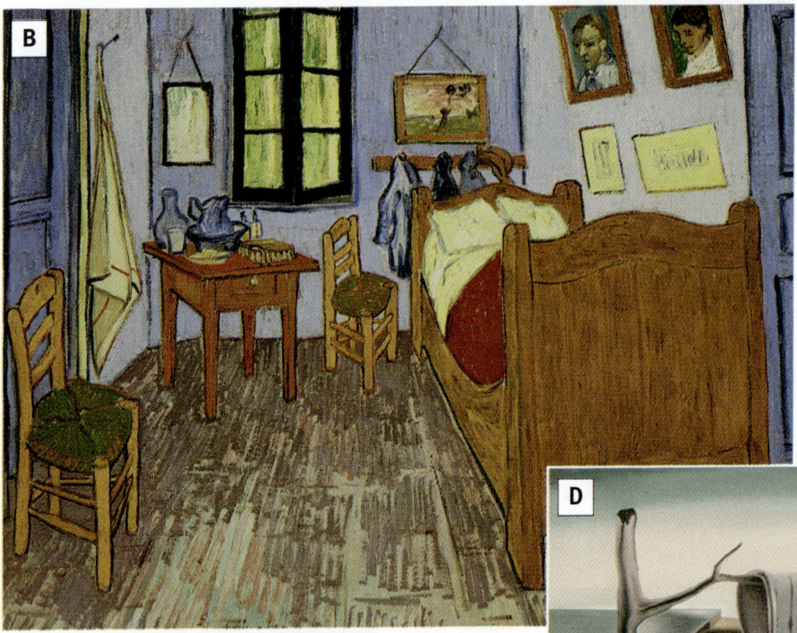

UNIT FOUR

C *this, that, these, those*

| this | that | these | those |

1 **Complete the conversations with *this, that, these,* or *those*.**

Doorman Tickets, please.
Woman G-34 and 35.
Doorman Sorry, ... is the wrong entrance. ....'s your entrance over there.

Woman Excuse me, ... are our seats.
Man J-34 and 35?
Woman No, ... are G-34 and 35. ....'s row J. .... are your seats over there.

2 **Listen and check.** (✱ 1.32)
Practise the conversations.

3 **Listen to the emphasis. Then practise.** (✱ 1.33)
Are these J-34 and 35? No, sorry, G-34 and 35.
Are these J-31 and 32? No, sorry, J-21 and 22.
Are these E-28 and 29? No, sorry, I-28 and 29.
Are these I-44 and 45? No, sorry, I-34 and 35.

D Modern art

▲ *Composition with red, yellow, and blue (1928)*

▶ *Four Campbell's soup cans (1965)*

1 **Complete the sentences.**
.... painting is .... the Dutch artist, Piet Mondrian.
.... 's in an art museum .... Germany. In the 1920s, Mondrian only used black, white, red, yellow, and blue.
.... four paintings are .... the American artist, Andy Warhol.
.... are in the Museum of Modern Art .... New York. Warhol used the wrong colours. Campbell's soup cans aren't pink, orange, green, blue, or purple. They're red and white.

Now listen and check. (✱ 1.34)

2 **Complete the spaces with question words.**
 1 '.................. is the painting by?' 'It's by Mondrian.'
 2 '.................. is the painting?' 'It's in Germany.'
 3 '.................. colours are in the painting?' 'Black, white, red, yellow, and blue.'

Ask and answer about the Warhol painting.

E Colours

1 Label the colours.

yellow   light blue   grey   pink   green   orange   white
purple   dark blue   black   red   brown

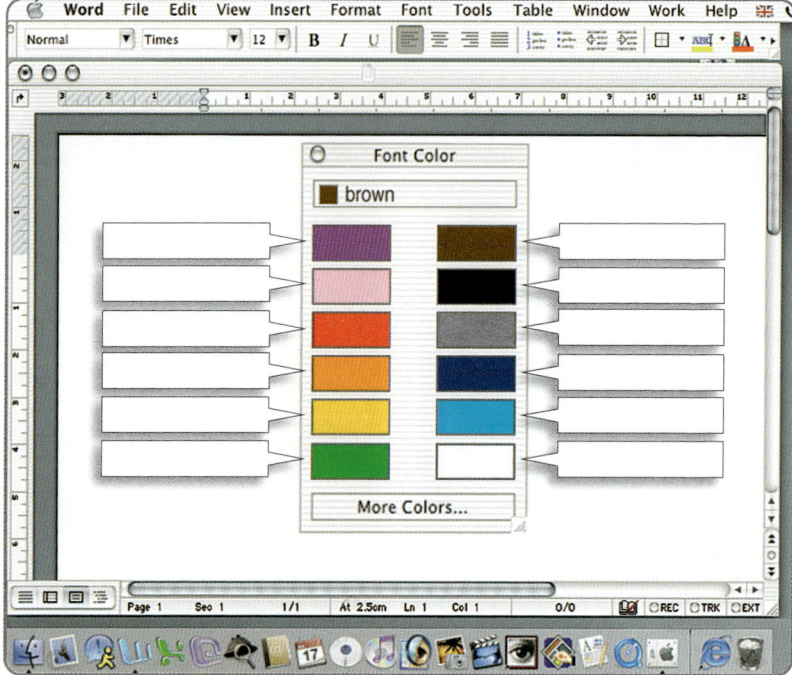

2 Ask and answer about flags and sports teams. (* 1.35)
- ▶ What colour is the American flag?
- ◀ It's red, white, and blue.
- ▶ What colour are Brazilian football shirts?
- ◀ They're yellow.

3 Can you add words to the colours?

red   A **red** card (in football), 'The **Reds**' (Manchester United), The **Red** Sea, **red** wine, **red** apples, **red** = angry, **red** = lucky (in China)

blue   green   white   black   grey   yellow   others

> The computer menu has the US spelling of **color**, while the text has the UK spelling, **colour**. Computer menus use the US spellings.

See **Extension 4** p.163

5 Have you got ...?

A What make?

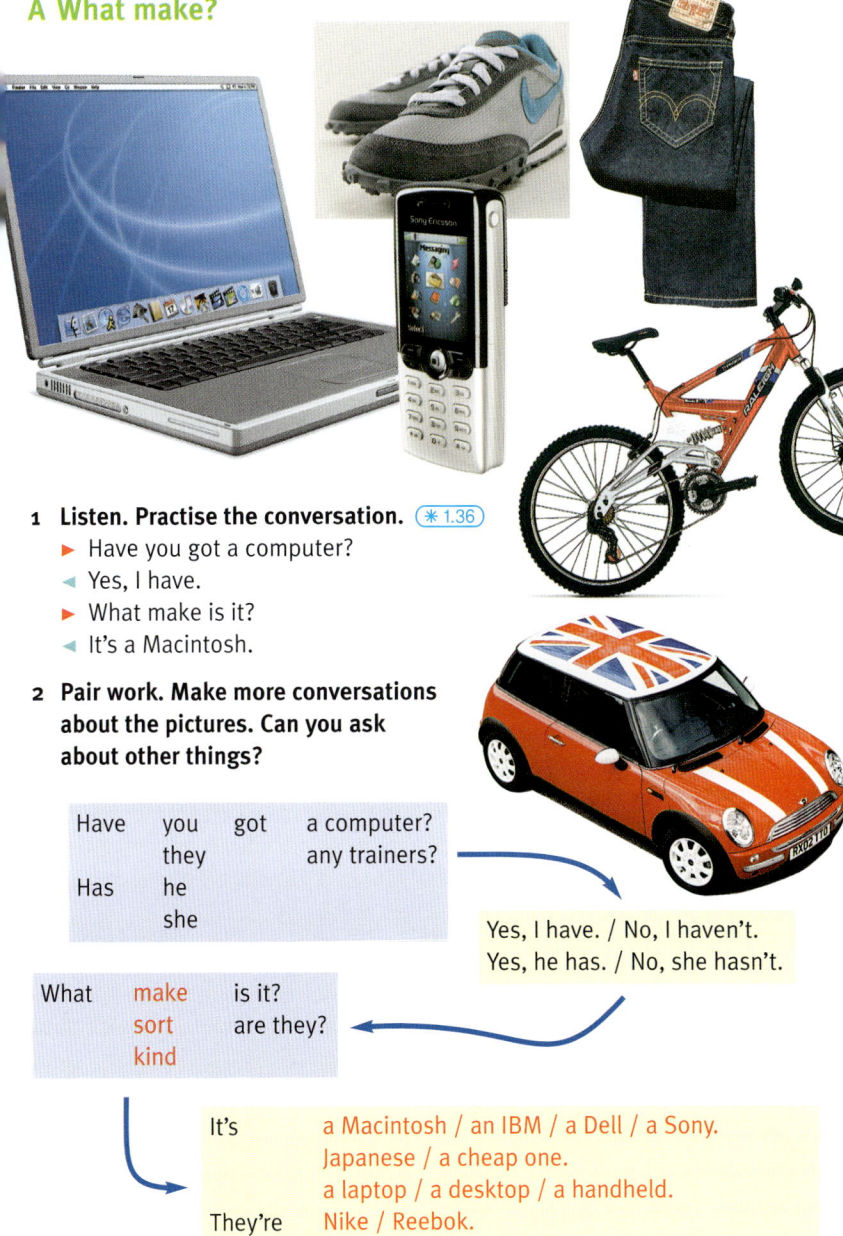

1 **Listen. Practise the conversation.** ✱ 1.36
   ▶ Have you got a computer?
   ◀ Yes, I have.
   ▶ What make is it?
   ◀ It's a Macintosh.

2 **Pair work. Make more conversations about the pictures. Can you ask about other things?**

Have	you	got	a computer?
	they		any trainers?
Has	he		
	she		

Yes, I have. / No, I haven't.
Yes, he has. / No, she hasn't.

What	make	is it?
	sort	are they?
	kind	

It's	a Macintosh / an IBM / a Dell / a Sony.
	Japanese / a cheap one.
	a laptop / a desktop / a handheld.
They're	Nike / Reebok.
I don't know.	

3 **Change partners. Ask about your first partner.**

B *have got / has got*

1 When do you use *have got / has got*? Add these words to the table.

| a girlfriend | a light (for a cigarette) | influenza | an umbrella |
| brown eyes | some jeans | | |

Possessions	a computer, some trainers
Describing people	black hair
Family and friends	a boyfriend
Illnesses	a headache
Idioms	the time

Can you add more words?

I / you / we / they **have** / **haven't got**   He / she / it **has** / **hasn't got**
Have I / you / we / they **got** ...?   **Has** he / she / it **got** ...?

Positive
I've got **some** trainers.

Negative, question
I haven't got **any** trainers.   Have you got **any** trainers?

2 Make sentences.

I've got brown hair and blue eyes.
I've got some new shoes.
I haven't got any aspirins.
I haven't got a headache.

3 Pronunciation.

There are two pronunciations of *have* and *has*.
Stressed (strong) form: have /hæv/, has /hæz/
Unstressed (weak) form: have /həv/, has /həz/
You needn't say the unstressed form, but you need to understand it when you are listening.

Listen and write S (stressed), or U (unstressed). ✳ 1.37

1 Have ☐ you got the time?
2 Yes, I have ☐. It's ten o'clock.
3 Have ☐ you got a light?
4 No, I haven't ☐. I don't smoke.
5 Has ☐ she got any children?
6 No, she hasn't ☐.

C Families

1 **Match the sentences with the same meaning.**

1 Has your sister got any sons?
2 Has your brother got any daughters?
3 Has your father got any sisters?
4 Has your mother got any brothers?
5 Has your uncle got any children?

A Have you got any aunts?
B Have you got any uncles?
C Have you got any nephews?
D Have you got any cousins?
E Have you got any nieces?

Now ask about your partner's family.

2 **Listen.** ✳ 1.38

▶ Have you got any brothers or sisters?
◀ No, I haven't. I'm an only child. What about you?
▶ I've got two brothers and a sister.
◀ Have you got any children?
▶ Yes, I've got two boys and a girl.

3 **Ask more questions about your partner's family.**
What's (*her name*)? What (*are their names*)?
How old (*is he*)? How old (*are they*)?

D Appointments

1 Days of the week. Listen and repeat. (✻ 1.39)

Monday   Tuesday   Wednesday   Thursday   Friday
Saturday   Sunday

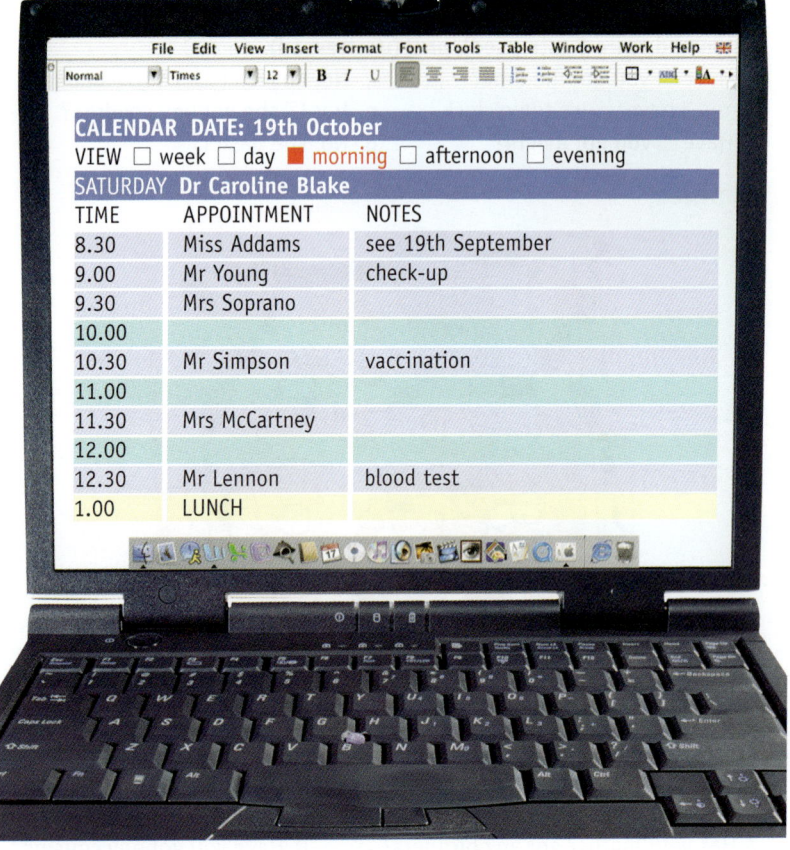

2 Listen. (✻ 1.40)

- ▶ Can I see Dr Blake?
- ◀ Have you got an appointment?
- ▶ No, I haven't.
- ◀ Well, she hasn't got any spaces *today*. How about *Saturday*?
- ▶ OK. What time?
- ◀ She's got a space at *ten o'clock*.
- ▶ Yes, that's fine.

3 Pair work. Practise the conversation. Change the words in *italics*.
this morning / this afternoon / this evening
Monday / Tuesday / Wednesday / Thursday / Friday
eleven o'clock / twelve o'clock / four o'clock

E What have you got?

SCENE 34: THE SALOON, DAY

LUKE OK, Stranger, what cards have you got?

STRANGER Four kings!

LUKE Miss Lucy?

LUCY Ten, jack, queen, king, and ace. (SMILES) It's my money, boys.

STRANGER Wait a minute! I've got four kings, and she's got a king. That ain't right. She's a cheat!

LUKE (STANDS UP) Go for your gun …

STRANGER I haven't got a gun.

LUKE Then go for a walk.

CUT

1 Listen. (✱ 1.41)

2 What is 's in these sentences? Is it *is* or *has*?
1 He's got four kings.
2 She's got a king.
3 It's her money.
4 She's a cheat.
5 Luke's got a gun.
6 Who's got four kings?

3 Practise the film script.

See **Extension 5** p.164

6 Work

A What's your job?

1 **Listen.** ✱1.42

My name's Cindy Grant. I'm a telephone operator. I work in a big hotel in London. I work 35 hours a week, and I work from Monday to Friday. I don't work at weekends.

2 **Listen to the questions. Tick (✓) the correct answers for Cindy.** ✱1.43

1 ☐ Yes, I have.   ☐ No, I haven't.
2 ☐ Yes, I do.   ☐ No, I don't.
3 ☐ Yes, I am.   ☐ No, I'm not.
4 ☐ Yes, I do.   ☐ No, I don't.
5 ☐ Yes, I do.   ☐ No, I don't.

3 **Complete the sentences.**
I'm a businessman. I work .... an office. I work 40 hours .... week, and I work .... Monday .... Friday. I don't work .... weekends.

B What do you do?

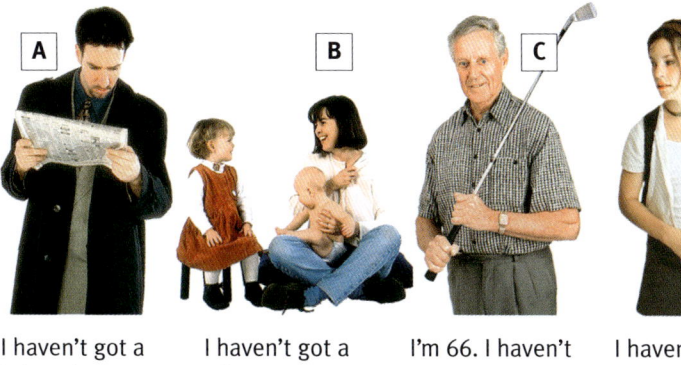

I haven't got a job at the moment. I'm ....

I haven't got a job. I've got two small children at home. I'm ....

I'm 66. I haven't got a job. I'm ....

I haven't got a job. I'm at university. I'm ....

1 **Complete the sentences with these words.**

   retired   a student   a full-time mother   unemployed

   Listen and check. (✱ 1.44)

2 **Match the jobs to the places. Can you add more?**

Job	Place
receptionist	office
teacher	shop
salesperson	hotel
clerk	factory
secretary	school
nurse	restaurant
waiter	bank
machine operator	hospital

   What's your job?
   I'm a nurse.   I haven't got a job.

   What do you do?
   I'm a nurse.   I'm retired.   I work in a factory.

3 **Pair work. Ask and answer.**
   1 What do you do?
   2 Where do you work?
   3 How many hours a week do you work?
   4 Do you work from Monday to Friday?
   5 Do you work at weekends?

C What does he do?

> John Hardy is a sales representative.
> He works for Vantax, a computer software company. The company makes computer games. John sells the games to shops. He doesn't work in an office, and he doesn't work regular hours. John travels about one thousand miles a week.

1 **Listen.** ✱ 1.45

2 **Answer with *Yes, he / it does.* or *No, he / it doesn't.***
   1 Does he work for a computer hardware company?
   2 Does the company make computers?
   3 Does he sell the games to shops?
   4 Does he work in an office?
   5 Does he work regular hours?
   6 Does he travel in his job?

3 **Ask and answer.**
   1 What does John do?
   2 Which company does he work for?
   3 What does his company make?

*I **work** in a hospital.*   *We **work** for a big company.*
*They **work** from nine to five.*
*He work**s** in a bank.*   *She work**s** for British Airways.*
*She work**s** at weekends.*

***Do** you **work** at home?*   *Yes, I **do**. / No, I **don't**.*
***Does** he **work** in an office?*   *Yes, he **does**. / No, he **doesn't**.*

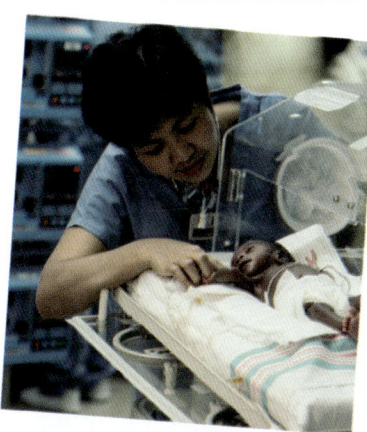

4 Choose the correct words.
1 What (does she / does she do)?
2 She's a nurse. She (work / works) in a hospital.
3 She doesn't (work / works) regular hours.
4 She (wear / wears) a blue uniform at work.
5 Does she (work / works) at night?

5 Complete the sentences with these words.

from   for   in   to   at

1 They're lab technicians. They work .... a science laboratory.
2 They work .... Chemex PLC.
3 They work regular hours, ... eight .... four thirty.
4 They don't work .... weekends.

D Game: asking questions

1 Read.
'What's my line?' is an old TV quiz game (*line* means job). The game was popular in countries all over the world. These are the rules:
- Four people guess someone's job. They ask questions, and the contestant answers with 'yes' or 'no'. When the contestant answers 'no', the next person asks a question.
- They can't ask *Wh-* questions (e.g. *What do you do? Where do you work?*).
- They ask questions until the contestant answers 'no' ten times.

2 Listen to 'What's my line?'. ✱ 1.46

3 What does he do? Can you guess? Listen and check. ✱ 1.47

4 Tick (✓) the questions you heard.
- ☐ Do you work in an office?
- ☐ Do you work from nine to five?
- ☐ Do you work inside?
- ☐ Do you wear a uniform?
- ☐ Do you meet people in your job?
- ☐ Have you got any qualifications?
- ☐ Have you got a university degree?
- ☐ Do you travel in your job?
- ☐ Do you work alone?
- ☐ Do you work at weekends?
- ☐ Do you sell something?
- ☐ Are you a footballer?

COMMUNICATION

Play 'What's my line?'. Two students are contestants.
Student A Look at Activity 2 on p.191.
Student B Look at Activity 14 on p.200.

5 Play the game. This time you choose the jobs.

See **Extension 6** p.165

7 Home

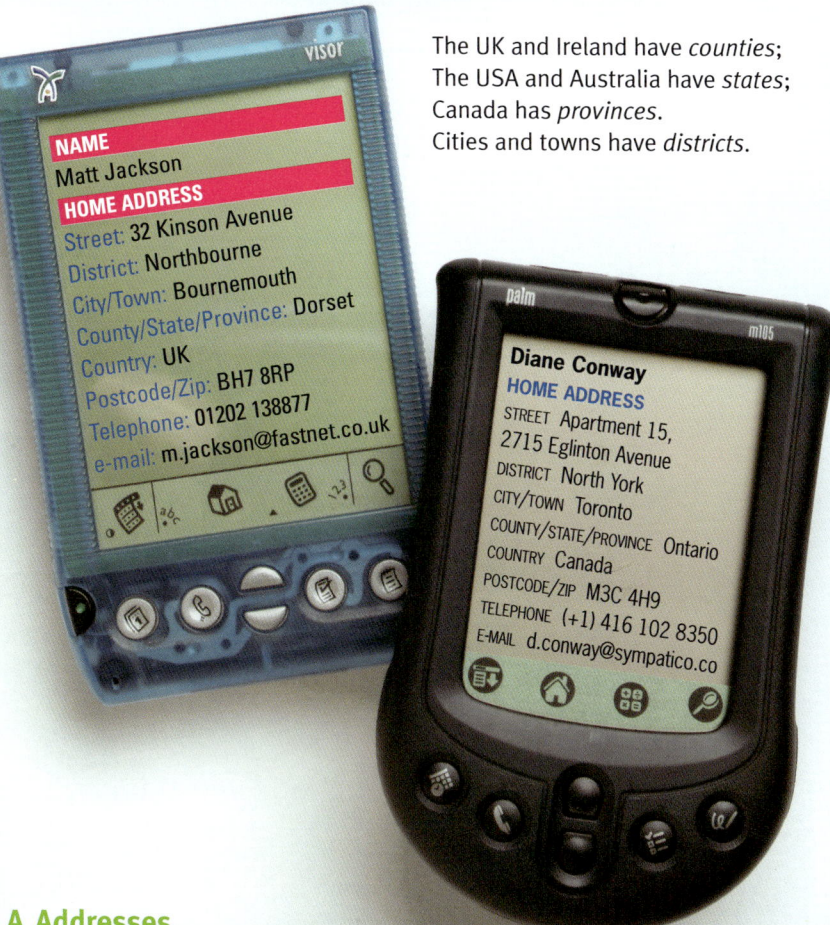

The UK and Ireland have *counties*;
The USA and Australia have *states*;
Canada has *provinces*.
Cities and towns have *districts*.

A Addresses

1 Look at the addresses, and listen to two conversations. There are three mistakes in each address. Correct them. ✱ 1.48 – 1.49

2 **Ask and answer about Matt.**
   What town does he live in?
   What county does he live in?
   What's his postcode?
   What's his e-mail address?

   Make more questions with:

   | district | street | country | phone number |

3 **Ask and answer about Diane.**

B Where do you live?

1 Label the things in the picture with these words.

> city   port   suburb   sea
> factories   airport   town
> country   beach   river   lake
> village   hills   mountains

UNIT SEVEN

We use **the** before the names of rivers, oceans, seas, and ranges of mountains: **The** *Mississippi*, **The** *Alps*, **The** *Atlantic*, **The** *Black Sea*.

We don't use an article (**a**, **an**, or **the**) before the names of cities, countries, single mountains or lakes: *Toronto, India, Mount Everest, Lake Ontario*.

I live in **the** *country* (opposite of *a city*).
Thailand is **a** *country in Asia.*

Chicago is on Lake Michigan.
Lake Michigan is large and famous.
Tom lives in Chicago. He lives near **the** *lake.*

Switzerland has many lakes. Heidi lives in Switzerland. She lives in **a** *village. It's near* **a** *small lake.*

2 **Complete with *a*, *the*, or no article (–).**
I live in .... Cape Town in .... South Africa. I'm lucky because I live near .... sea and near .... Table Mountain. There's .... supermarket near my house, and .... cinema too. I go to .... University of Cape Town. I'm .... law student. My home is about fifty kilometres from .... Cape of Good Hope, where .... Atlantic Ocean meets .... Indian Ocean.

Listen and check. (✱ 1.50)

3 **Pair work. Ask and answer.**
▶ Do you live in (a city / a town / a suburb / the country)?
◀ (Yes, I do. / No, I don't.)
▶ Do you live near (the city centre / the mountains / the sea / a beach / an airport / a lake / a river)?
◀ (Yes, I do. / No, I don't.)

4 **Change partners. Ask about your first partner.**

SOUTHAMPTON

City • County: Hampshire • South of England
70 miles from London • Population: 250,000

Southampton is a port. The ships the 'Mayflower' (1620) and the 'Titanic' (1912) sailed from Southampton docks. The 'Mayflower' took the first English emigrants to North America. There's a 'Mayflower' memorial, and there are two 'Titanic' memorials in the city. Southampton still has some city walls, and the old city gate (Bargate), but it's also a modern city. There are two universities, three shopping malls, two multiplex cinemas, two theatres, several international hotels, a marina, and an international airport. West Quay Shopping Centre is the largest city-centre mall in the south of England. There's an art gallery, and there are several museums. Southampton FC is the local football club, and it has a modern stadium. Cruise ships depart from the docks. Southampton hasn't got a cathedral and it hasn't got a major concert hall. There aren't any beaches in Southampton.

C Southampton

1 Listen and read. Label the photos of Southampton. ✱ 1.51

| Marina | West Quay | Docks | Bargate |

2 Read again, and underline ten places.

stadium, docks

Make sentences with:

| There is (*a* / *an*) ... | There isn't (*a* / *an*) ... |
| There are (*some* / *three*) ... | There aren't any ... |

There **is** (*a cinema*). There **isn't** (*a supermarket*).
There **are** (*some* / *four* / *several* / *lots of*) hotels.
There **aren't** (*any* / *many*) factories.
Is there (*a marina*)? Yes, there **is**. / No, there **isn't**.
Are there (*any museums*)? Yes, there **are**. / No, there **aren't**.

3 **Ask and answer.**
How many theatres are there?
How many shopping malls are there?
How many multiplex cinemas are there?
How many universities are there?
How many museums are there?

4 **Choose the correct words.**
1 Is (it / there) an international airport in Southampton?
2 Are there (any / a) shopping malls?
3 There (isn't / aren't) a cathedral.
4 There (is / are) two theatres.
5 There are (two / any) multiplex cinemas.
6 There are (many / several) museums.

5 **Close your books. Ask your partner five questions about Southampton.**

D About your town

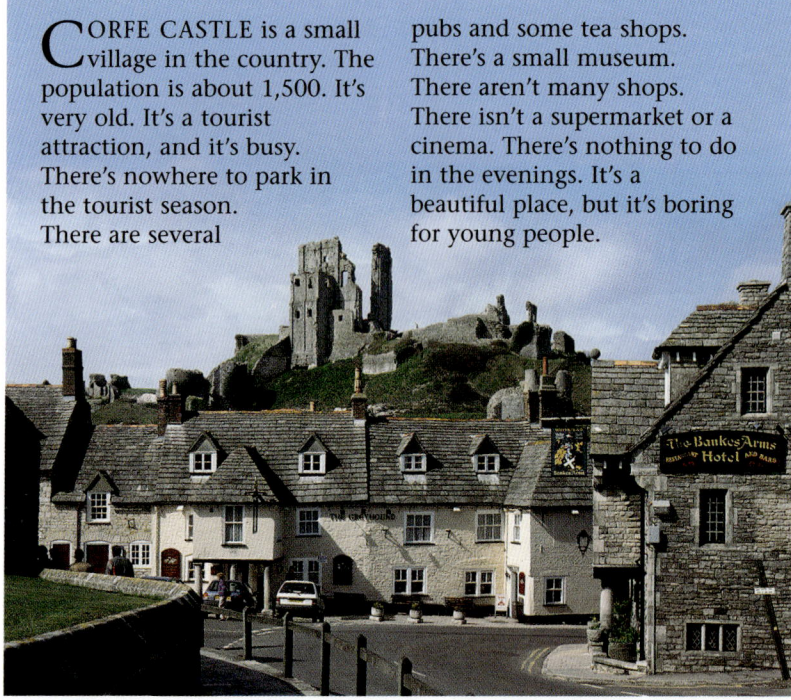

CORFE CASTLE is a small village in the country. The population is about 1,500. It's very old. It's a tourist attraction, and it's busy. There's nowhere to park in the tourist season. There are several pubs and some tea shops. There's a small museum. There aren't many shops. There isn't a supermarket or a cinema. There's nothing to do in the evenings. It's a beautiful place, but it's boring for young people.

1 **Read about the village of Corfe Castle in England.** ✱ 1.52

2 **Pair work. Ask and answer.**
   ► Is your *(town)* large or small?
   ◄ It's *(large)*.
   ► What's the population?
   ◄ It's about *(two hundred thousand)*. / I don't know.

   | 200 – two hundred   2,000 – two thousand   20,000 – twenty thousand
   | 200,000 – two hundred thousand   2,000,000 – two million

3 **How many true sentences can you make about your town? Use these words.**
   cinema   supermarket   football stadium   beach   theatre
   concert hall   church   cathedral   shopping mall   shop   park
   factory   airport

4 **Tick (✓) the adjectives that describe the place where you live.**
   ☐ large   ☐ small   ☐ old   ☐ modern   ☐ busy   ☐ quiet
   ☐ important   ☐ beautiful

   Now talk about the place where you live. What are the good things? What are the bad things?

   See **Extension 7** p.166

8 Travel

A Flight arrivals

```
ARRIVALS LHR Terminal 3    TIME NOW: 19.12

time    flight   from              status
19.35   TG916    Bangkok           Expected 19.15
19.35   VS604    Cape Town         Expected 19.25
20.00   VS018    Newark            On time
20.20   AA142    New York          On time
20.50   AA156    Boston            Expected 20.45
21.10   AC868    Toronto           Expected 21.23
21.15   UA976    New York          On time
22.35   AA090    Chicago           Expected 22.55
```

1 **Listen. Which flight are they talking about?** (✷ 1.53)

2 **Listen and repeat these times.** (✷ 1.54)
   06.05   07.10   08.15   09.20   10.25   11.30   12.35
   13.40   14.45   15.50   16.55   17.00   18.32   19.07

3 **Pair work. Ask and answer. Change the words in *italics*.** (✷ 1.55)
   ▶ What time does *VS604* arrive?
   ◀ From *Cape Town*?
   ▶ Yes.
   ◀ It arrives at *nineteen twenty-five*. It's *early*.

   early / on time / late

B Train departures

1. **What have they got? Listen and tick (✓) the boxes.** (✱ 1.56)
   - ☐ passports
   - ☐ money
   - ☐ tickets
   - ☐ hotel vouchers
   - ☐ credit cards
   - ☐ seat reservations
   - ☐ paper tissues
   - ☐ magazines
   - ☐ sandwiches

2. **Listen and find the answers.** (✱ 1.57)
   What time is it now?
   What time does their train leave?
   Which platform does it leave from?
   Where are they going?
   How many minutes have they got before the train leaves?

Waterloo International *eurostar*

Train No.	9010	9116	9012	9014	9074
London Waterloo	8.23	8.27	8.53	9.23	9.27
Ashford International	9.23	9.27		10.23	10.27
Lille-Europe		11.29	11.51		
Disneyland® Paris					13.29
Paris (Gare du Nord)	12.23		12.53		
Brussels		12.10		13.23	

3. **Pair work. Ask and answer about the timetable. It's 9.00 a.m.** (✱ 1.58)
   - ▶ What time does the next train to Brussels leave?
   - ◀ It leaves at 9.23.
   - ▶ Does it stop at Lille?
   - ◀ No, it doesn't.
   - ▶ What time does it arrive in Brussels?
   - ◀ It arrives at 13.23.

C Bus times

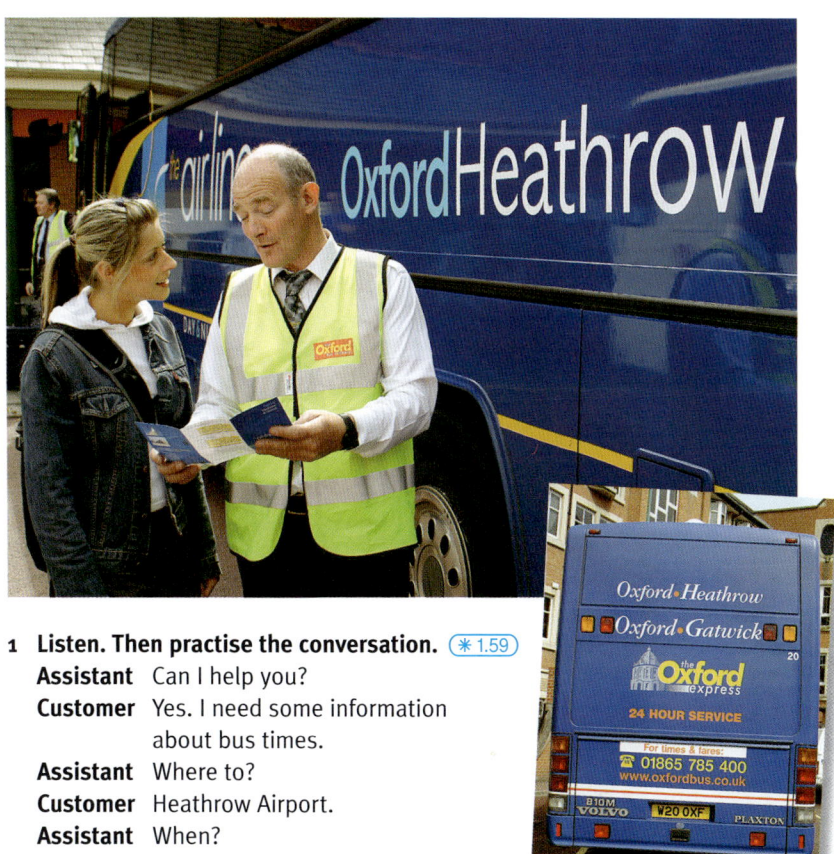

1 Listen. Then practise the conversation. ✱ 1.59

Assistant Can I help you?
Customer Yes. I need some information about bus times.
Assistant Where to?
Customer Heathrow Airport.
Assistant When?
Customer Tomorrow.
Assistant What time?
Customer About ten o'clock. My check-in time's twelve thirty.
Assistant There's one at ten fifteen.
Customer What time does it get to the airport?
Assistant Twelve oh five.
Customer That's fine. Thank you.

2 Make conversations with this information.

BUS TIMETABLE
Departures to Heathrow Airport

departs	09.00	10.15	11.30	12.45
arrives	11.10	12.05	13.20	14.35

3 Match the times.

half past eleven — 11.05
a quarter to twelve — 11.45
a quarter past eleven — 11.25
five past eleven — 11.30
eleven o'clock — 11.40
twenty to twelve — 11.50
twenty-five past eleven — 11.15
ten to twelve — 11.00

D Your journey to work

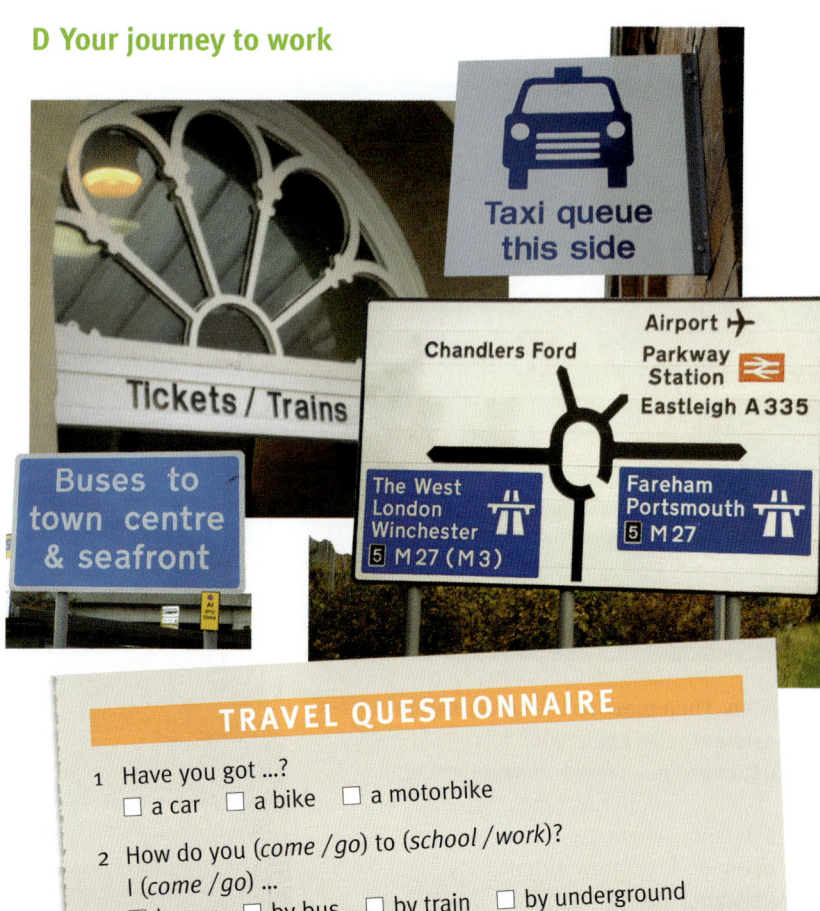

TRAVEL QUESTIONNAIRE

1 Have you got …?
   ☐ a car   ☐ a bike   ☐ a motorbike

2 How do you (*come / go*) to (*school / work*)?
   I (*come / go*) …
   ☐ by car   ☐ by bus   ☐ by train   ☐ by underground
   ☐ by taxi   ☐ by bike ☐ walk

3 How long does it take?
   ☐ ten minutes   ☐ half an hour   ☐ an hour
   ☐ two hours   ☐ other

4 What time do you leave home? ▭

5 What time do you get to (*school / work*)? ▭

1 Read the questionnaire.

2 Listen. Which questions are these people answering?
   Write the question numbers. (✱1.60)
   A ☐   B ☐   C ☐   D ☐   E ☐

3 Interview your partner and complete the questionnaire.
   Compare the results for the class.

See **Extension 8** p.167

9 Instructions

A Be careful!

A

B

C

D

E

F

1 **Where can you find these signs?**
   in an American street   on the beach   by a railway   on an old house by an American crossroads   near the sea

2 **Listen. Match the conversations to the signs.**

   ✻ 1.61 ☐   ✻ 1.62 ☐   ✻ 1.63 ☐
   ✻ 1.64 ☐   ✻ 1.65 ☐   ✻ 1.66 ☐

B Instructions

1 .... 2 .... 3 .... 4 ....

5 .... 6 .... 7 .... 8 ....

1 Label the signs with these words.

> Be careful.   Don't smoke.   Turn right.   Don't turn left.
> Turn left.   Don't eat or drink.   Don't drop litter.   Stop.

2 Pronunciation. Listen to these sentences.
Tick (✓) the sentences that sound friendly.
Put a cross (X) by the sentences that don't sound friendly. ✶1.67
   1 Please be careful.
   2 Please be careful.
   3 Shh. Don't talk. Be quiet.
   4 Be quiet, please.
   5 Don't look at her, look at me.
   6 Please sit down.
   7 Open the window, please.
   8 Don't sit there, sit here.

> Adding **please** makes sentences more polite, but you can say *Be quiet, please* or *Be quiet* in a friendly way or an unfriendly way. The sound of your voice is the important thing.

3 Say the sentences in a friendly, polite way.
Then say them in an unfriendly way.

4 Match the opposites.

   1 Come in.   A Turn it off.
   2 Stand up.   B Pull.
   3 Turn it on.   C Be quiet.
   4 Open your book.   D Go out.
   5 Push.   E Put it down.
   6 Talk.   F Take your coat off.
   7 Pick it up.   G Close your book.
   8 Put your coat on.   H Sit down.

C Look at me!

Subject pronouns	I	you	he	she	it	we	they
Possessive adjectives	my	your	his	her	its	our	their
Object pronouns	me	you	him	her	it	us	them

1 Complete with object pronouns.

'Pick .... up, please.'

'Don't wear your football boots in the house. Take .... off.'

'Aah, isn't he sweet! Look at .... !'

'Take a photograph of ....'

'This is your Aunt Nellie. Kiss ....'

'Hey, Mum! Look at ....'

2 Pronunciation. Listen and copy the emphasis. (✱ 1.68)
This isn't for me, it's for her.
They aren't for us, they're for them.
That isn't for her, it's for him.
Those aren't for you, they're for us.
It isn't for him, it's for you.

3 Give your partner instructions.
Look at me. Don't laugh. Open your book. Close your book. Take off your watch. Give it to me. Stand up. Go to the door. Open it. Close it. Turn on the light. Turn off the light. Come here. Don't sit down. Stand there. Thank you.

D Smile!

1 Listen to the photographer. ✳ 1.69

2 Listen again. Number the players on the diagram. Listen and check. ✳ 1.70

UNIT NINE

3 Complete the sentences with these words.

> behind   on the left   middle
> in front of   back   between
> on the right   front

1 Number 9 is .... number 4 and number 7.
2 Number 8 is .... number 11.
3 Number 3 is .... number 10.
4 Number 4 is in the .... row.
5 Number 10 is in the .... row.
6 Number 6 is in the .... row.
7 Number 1 is .... of number 11.
8 Number 9 is .... of number 4.

4 Talk about your class.
Who is behind you?
Who is on your right?
Who is in front of you?
Who is on your left?

5 Work in groups. One is the photographer. The others are in rows. Put people in position for your photograph.

See **Extension 9** p.168

10 Can and can't

A Abilities

1 Match the words.

run	under water
swim	a tank
ride	a cake
drive	a marathon
play	the guitar
make	a horse

2 Listen and read. (✳ 1.71)

run?   100 metres / 1,500 metres / a marathon
- ▶ Can you run?
- ◀ Yes, of course I can.
- ▶ Can you run 100 metres?
- ◀ Yes, I can.
- ▶ Can you run 1500 metres?
- ◀ I don't know. Yes, I think I can.
- ▶ Can you run a marathon?
- ◀ No, I can't.

3 Pair work. Ask questions until you get a *no* answer. Can you add more examples?

swim?
swim underwater / swim underwater with your clothes on /
swim underwater with your clothes and shoes on

drive?
a car / a truck / a bus / a tank

play?
a musical instrument / the piano / the guitar / the drums / the saxophone

cook?
make an omelette / make a pizza / make a cake / make a wedding cake

ride?
a bike / a motorbike / a horse / an elephant

B Pronunciation

There are two pronunciations of *can*. (✳ 1.72)

stressed: can /kæn/   Yes, I can. Yes, they can.
unstressed: can /kən/   I can swim. Can you speak Spanish?

You needn't say the unstressed form, but you need to understand it when you are listening.

can't can be pronounced /kɑːnt/ or /kænt/.
Southern British English is /kɑːnt/.   I can't swim. No, I can't.
American and Northern British English is /kænt/.   I can't swim. No, I can't.

Listen and repeat. Then underline the sounds you hear.

1 Can you use Microsoft Word?   (/kən/ or /kæn/)
2 Yes, I can.   (/kən/ or /kæn/)
3 Can you program a computer?   (/kən/ or /kæn/)
4 No, I can't.   (/kɑːnt/ or /kænt/)
5 Can you play the guitar?   (/kən/ or /kæn/)
6 No, I can't.   (/kɑːnt/ or /kænt/)

Listen again and check.

C Listening

1 **Read the letter. Then listen to the four parts of the conversation. While you listen, tick (✓) Aunt Jemima's allergies.** ✱ 1.73 – 1.76
   ☐ dogs ☐ roses ☐ cheese
   ☐ potatoes ☐ meat ☐ bread
   ☐ nuts ☐ tea ☐ coffee
   ☐ ice-cream ☐ chocolate

> Dear David and Victoria,
> Thank you for the invitation. Yes, I can come to lunch on Sunday. See you at 12. Don't come to the station. I can get a taxi to your house.
> Best wishes
> Aunt Jemima

2 **Part one. Complete the sentences.**
   1 Is that your .... ?
   2 I can't go .... a dog!
   3 Take it .... !

   Listen and check. ✱ 1.73

3 **Part two. Listen and choose the correct words.** ✱ 1.74
   1 I (can / can't) sit outside.
   2 (I've got / I get) hay fever.
   3 We (can / can't) go into the dining room.
   4 (They're / There are) flowers on the table.
   5 Take (it / them) away.

4 Part three. Listen, then make true sentences from the chart. ✱1.75

| She | can
can't | eat cheese
eat potatoes
eat meat | because | she's a vegetarian.
she's allergic to it.
she's on a diet. |

5 Part four. Listen. ✱1.76
Ask and answer.
1 What things can't she eat?
2 What things can't she drink?
3 What can't she wear?
4 Can she eat ice-cream?
5 Why can't she eat chocolate ice-cream?

COMMUNICATION
Work in groups of four.
Student A Look at Activity 3 on p.191.
Student B Look at Activity 9 on p.196.
Student C Look at Activity 15 on p.200.
Student D Look at Activity 20 on p.204.

D 'You are what you eat.'
Discuss.
What things can't you eat? What things can't you drink? Why not?
Are you allergic to anything? If so, what are you allergic to?
What's your favourite food? Do you eat it every day?
What's your favourite foreign food?
Can you cook? What's your best recipe?

See **Extension 10** p.169

11 Is there any water?

A What's in your fridge?

UNIT ELEVEN

1 **Find these things in the picture.**

Group 1
pizzas   strawberries   peas
sardines   beans   cans of beer
sausages   potatoes

Group 2
cheese   milk   cat
food   steak   mineral
water   salad

What's the difference between the words in group 1 and group 2?
Complete the sentences. Use one word from group 1, and
one word from group 2.
There are some ....
There's some ....

2 **Look at the picture. Whose food is it? Guess.
There are four things for each person.**

Mark   Joan   James   Helen

Mark's fridge	....	....	....	....
Joan's fridge	....	....	....	....
James's fridge	....	....	....	....
Helen's fridge	....	....	....	....

Listen and check. (✳ 1.77 – 1.80)

3 **Ask and answer.**

possessive 's
his book → *Mark's book / James's book*
her book → *Helen's book / Joan's*

▶ Whose cheese is it?
◀ It's James's cheese.

▶ Whose sausages are they?
◀ They're Mark's sausages.

4 **Write a list of six things in your fridge. Ask about your partner's list.**
▶ Is there any cheese ?
◀ Yes, there is. / No, there isn't.

▶ Are there any sausages ?
◀ Yes, there are. / No, there aren't.

B Countable and uncountable

Countable
There are some / There aren't any / Are there any ...?

potatoes · grapes · vegetables
eggs · chips · chocolates
peas  · beans  · nuts 

pieces of + **uncountable**

slices of bread
pieces /əv/ meat

spoonfuls of sugar
grams /əv/ sugar
grains of rice
kilos /əv/ flour
cans of beer
litres /əv/ water
glasses /əv/ milk
bottles /əv/ wine

Uncountable
There is some / There isn't any / Is there any ...?

mashed potato  · sweetcorn  · pasta  · fruit
sugar  · rice  · flour 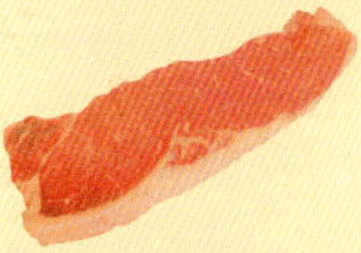 · meat 
bread  · chocolate  · cheese  · fish 
water  · milk  · wine  · salad

UNIT ELEVEN

1 English nouns are countable or uncountable. Dictionaries use the symbols [C] and [U] for countable and uncountable.

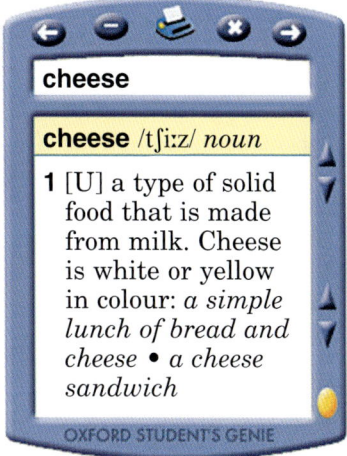
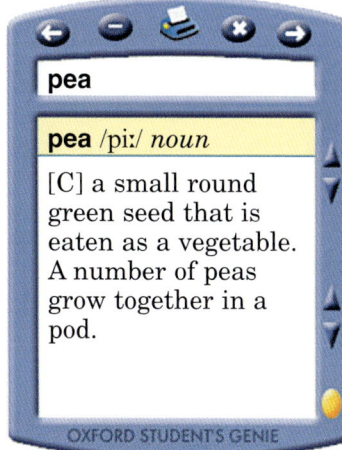

2 Look at the chart. Answer the questions.
1. All the words in the green box have plural -s endings. True or false?
2. None of the words in the yellow box have plural -s endings. True or false?
3. Can you count grapes?
4. Can you count grains of flour?
5. Does your language have countable and uncountable nouns?
6. Are they the same as the words on the chart?

3 Complete the sentences with *is, isn't, are,* or *aren't*.
1. Sorry, there .... any cheese in the fridge.
2. .... there any grapes in the fridge?
3. There .... some eggs in the fridge.
4. There .... some mashed potato in the bowl.
5. .... there any milk, please?
6. There .... any chips in the freezer.
7. This tea .... cold. Can I have another cup?
8. There .... 4.5 litres in a British gallon.

Some words are countable or uncountable.
*Can I have two **coffees**, please?* = [C]
***Is** there **any coffee** in the pot?* = [U]
*How **much is** the instant **coffee**? **It's** three fifty.* = [U]

4 These are words from units 1 to 10. Are they countable or uncountable? Put *C* or *U*.
- ☐ orange juice
- ☐ orange
- ☐ butter
- ☐ sandwich
- ☐ can of tuna
- ☐ tuna
- ☐ spaghetti
- ☐ burger
- ☐ soup
- ☐ croissant
- ☐ potato
- ☐ tomato

C Air miles

1 Listen and read. (✱ 1.81)

British supermarkets sell food from all over the world. Butter comes from New Zealand, and apples come from Australia. Beef comes from Argentina, and mangoes come from Brazil. They all come by sea.

Food imports to Britain

Food	Country	Air miles
fresh fish	Sri Lanka	5,500
asparagus	Thailand	6,000
peas	Zimbabwe	4,500
grapes	South Africa	6,200
sweetcorn	Peru	6,500
fresh tuna	Ecuador	6,000
Pacific salmon	Alaska, USA	4,700
strawberries	California, USA	5,500
mushrooms	China	6,000
tomatoes	Saudi Arabia	3,500

In Britain local asparagus is in the shops in May and June, but nowadays people want fresh asparagus all through the year. So Britain imports asparagus by air from Peru, Mexico, and Thailand. Fresh fish comes to Britain from Sri Lanka, Alaska, and Ecuador. Vegetables come from Zambia, Zimbabwe, and Kenya in East Africa. Grapes come from South Africa.

Ecologists measure 'air miles': the distance food travels by air from the producer to the shop. Because transport by air uses fuel, they say that 'air miles' food is bad for the environment.

2 Underline *come* and *comes* in the text.

3 Ask and answer about the food in the table.
Stressed form: Where do they come from /frɒm/?
Unstressed form: They come from /frəm/ Italy.

▶ Where do peas come from?
◀ They come from Zimbabwe.
▶ How many miles do they travel?
◀ They travel about 4,500 miles.

▶ Where does fresh tuna come from?
◀ It comes from Ecuador.
▶ How many miles does it travel?
◀ It travels about 6,000 miles.

4 Make two lists.

MY COUNTRY IMPORTS ...	MY COUNTRY EXPORTS ...
....	....

Talk about your country.
Rice comes from the USA. Apples come from France.
Fish goes to Spain. Strawberries go to Britain.

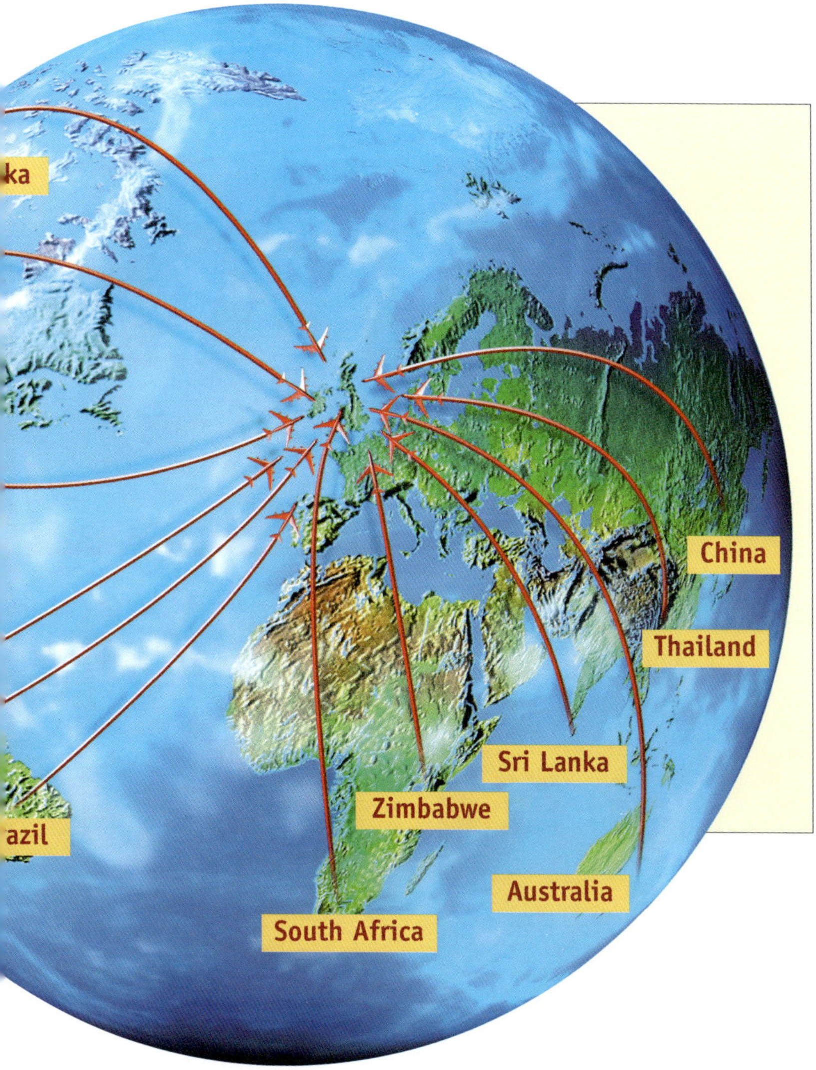

UNIT ELEVEN

China
Thailand
Sri Lanka
Zimbabwe
Australia
South Africa

See **Extension 11** p.170

12 I'd like ...

A What would you like?

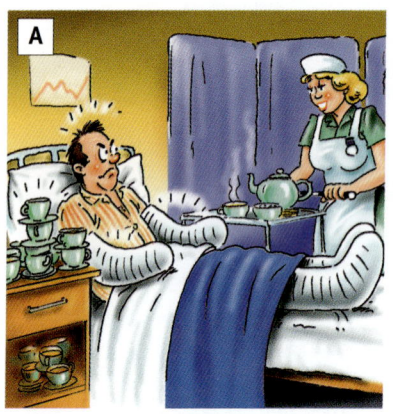

1 Listen. Match the conversations with the pictures.

✱ 1.82 ☐
- How much sugar would you like?
- Four spoonfuls, please.

✱ 1.83 ☐
- Would he like another one?
- No, he wouldn't, thank you!

✱ 1.84 ☐
- Would you like some tea, Mr Jones?
- No, thank you.

✱ 1.85 ☐
- I'd like some of those, please.
- How many would you like?

UNIT TWELVE   63

2 Complete the conversations with questions from the box. Then listen and check.

> A How many would you like?   D Would you like some airmail stickers?
> B Have you got any stamps?   E Have you got any ice?
> C How much would you like?   F Have you got any tickets for tonight?

(✱ 1.86)
- Festival Theatre. Booking office.
- Hello. ....
- Yes, we have. ....
- Two, please. Have you got any at the front?
- Sorry, we haven't. We've got some in the middle for 37.50, or at the back for 33.50.
- I'd like two in the middle, please.
- Right. Row K. Seats 37 and 38. That's 75 euros altogether.

(✱ 1.87)
- I'd like an orange juice, please.
- There you go.
- It isn't very cold. ....
- There's some in the ice-bucket. ....
- A lot, please!

(✱ 1.88)
- I'd like these postcards, please.
- They're 50 cents each. That's 2.50 altogether.
- Thanks. ....
- Yes. Where for?
- I'd like three for Europe, and two for the USA.
- There you go. ....
- Yes, please.

---

*I'd like **some tickets**.   I'd like **some ice**.*
*Would you like **some coffee**?*
Yes, I would. / Yes, please.   No, I wouldn't. / No, thank you.

countable: *How **many tickets** would you like?*
uncountable: *How **much ice** would you like?*

We use **any** with questions: *Have you got **any** mineral water?*
We use **some** with offers: *Would you like **some** mineral water?*

3 Practise the conversations in 2.

B Which one?

1 Make sentences with words from the box.

| gold silver plastic metal orange |
| purple pink blue large small |
| car house old new |

There's a pink ring binder.
There are some house keys.

2 Ask and answer about things in the picture.
- ▶ Which (*pen*) would you like?
- ◀ I'd like the (*gold*) one.
- ▶ Which (*sunglasses*) would you like?
- ◀ I'd like the (*metal*) ones.

3 Group work. Each student puts two or three things on the table. Ask about the things.
- ▶ Which is (*Anna's*) pen?
- ◀ The (*silver*) one.
- ▶ Which are (*Paul's*) keys?
- ◀ The (*Toyota*) ones.

4 Ask for things.
- ▶ Can I have (*Anna's book*), please?
- ◀ Which one is (*Anna's book*)?
- ▶ That one.
- ◀ Which one?
- ▶ The (*old*) one.

C Choices

1 Nowadays there are too many choices. Listen. (✱ 1.89)

2 Listen again. Tick (✓) his choices.

☐ cappuccino ☐ espresso ☐ latte ☐ Americano ☐ macchiato
☐ hot ☐ iced
☐ Colombian ☐ Brazilian ☐ Mexican ☐ Kenyan ☐ Blue Mountain ☐ Indonesian
☐ regular ☐ decaffeinated
☐ white ☐ black
☐ cream ☐ milk ☐ half and half
☐ full-fat milk ☐ half-fat milk ☐ low-fat milk
☐ brown sugar ☐ white sugar ☐ low-calorie sweetener
☐ small ☐ regular ☐ large ☐ extra large
☐ drink here ☐ take out

3 Role play. Act out a conversation at the airport coffee stand.

See **Extension 12** p.171

13 Shopping in London

Oxford Street is the main shopping street in London's West End. It runs from Marble Arch in the west to Tottenham Court Road in the east. The Central Line of the London underground ('the tube') has four stations along Oxford Street. There are several large department stores, including Selfridges, which is the biggest store in Britain. You can find many international shops in Oxford Street, like HMV, Borders bookshop, Virgin Megastore, and Topshop. Regent Street and New Bond Street are also worth a visit. The famous Liberty store is in Regent Street. If you're looking for designer clothes, Bond Street is the place for you.

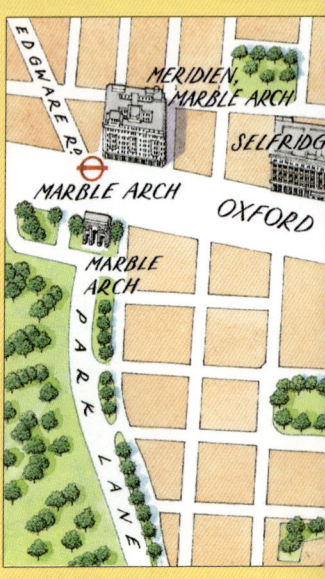

A Oxford Street

1 **Listen and read.** ✱ 1.90

2 **Find the places on the map.**

3 **The speakers are outside the Meridien Hotel. Listen and practise the conversations.**
   ✱ 1.91
   - Excuse me ...
   - Yes?
   - I'm looking for Bond Street station.
   - Go along Oxford Street. Go past Selfridges, and it's on the right.

   ✱ 1.92
   - I'm looking for Liberty. Do you know it?
   - Yes. Go along Oxford Street to Oxford Circus, and turn right into Regent Street. It's on the left.

UNIT THIRTEEN

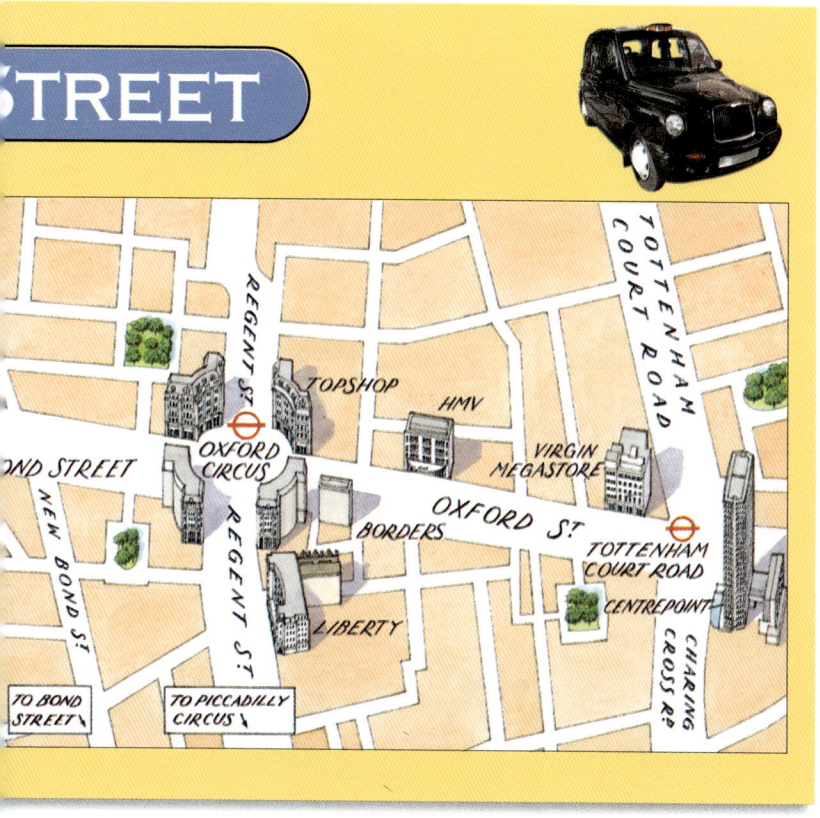

(✱ 1.93)

- Excuse me, where's the Virgin Megastore?
- It's at the other end of Oxford Street, near Tottenham Court Road station.
- Is it far?
- You can walk there in about thirty minutes, or you can take the tube or a bus.

(✱ 1.94)

- Can you help me? I'm looking for Selfridges.
- Mmm. It's not far. It's along here on the left. You can't miss it.

(✱ 1.95)

- Excuse me, I'm trying to find the Meridien Hotel.
- Sorry, I can't help you. I'm a stranger here myself.

4 **Pair work. Choose a place on the map (e.g. Oxford Circus). Ask directions to other places.**

B Department store

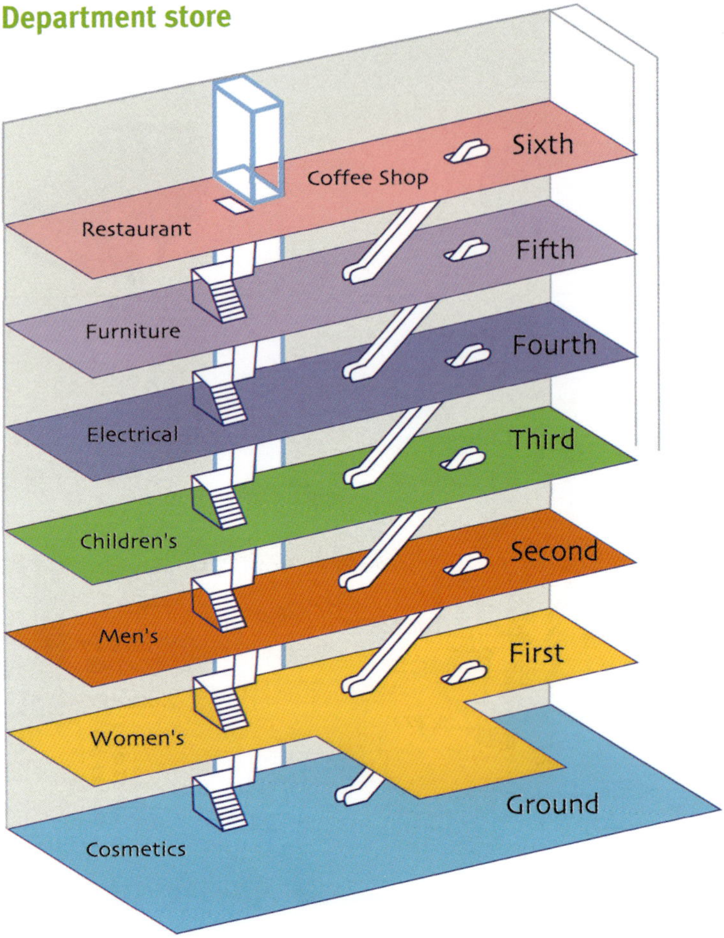

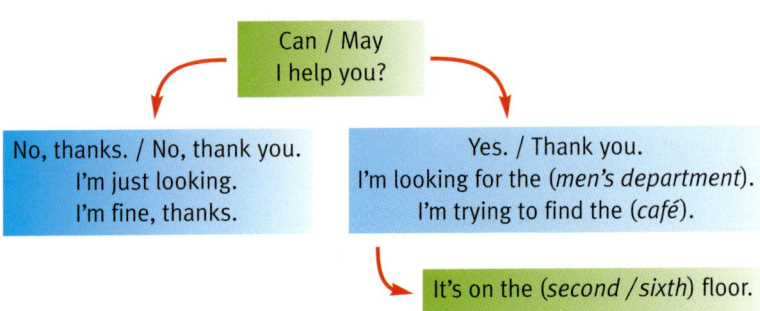

1. **Listen. Find the two conversations.** (✱ 1.96)

   Can / May I help you?

   → No, thanks. / No, thank you. I'm just looking. I'm fine, thanks.

   → Yes. / Thank you. I'm looking for the (*men's department*). I'm trying to find the (*café*).

   → It's on the (*second / sixth*) floor.

2. **Pronunciation. Say:**
   the /ð/ four**th** /θ/ floor   **th**e fif**th** floor   **th**e six**th** floor

3. **Pair work. Make conversations with information on the store guide.**

C Music store

1 Listen and practise. They're on the ground floor. (✱ 1.97)

Assistant Are you finding everything OK?
Man I'm looking for the rock section.
Assistant It's upstairs on the first floor.
Man Thanks.

2 Look at the store guide. You're on the ground floor. Make conversations.

3 Listen. Then answer the questions. (✱ 1.98)
1 What's he looking for?
2 Who's the artist?
3 Has the store got it?
4 Can the store get it?
5 How much is it?

D Song

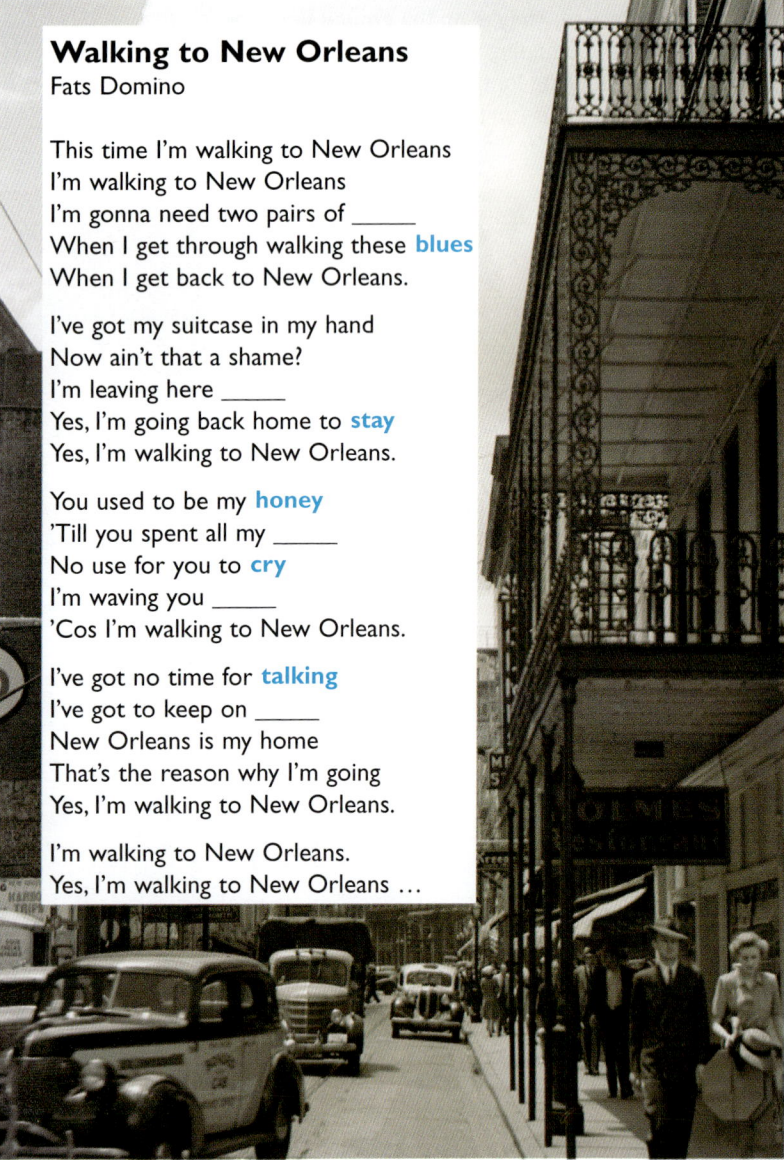

Walking to New Orleans
Fats Domino

This time I'm walking to New Orleans
I'm walking to New Orleans
I'm gonna need two pairs of _____
When I get through walking these **blues**
When I get back to New Orleans.

I've got my suitcase in my hand
Now ain't that a shame?
I'm leaving here _____
Yes, I'm going back home to **stay**
Yes, I'm walking to New Orleans.

You used to be my **honey**
'Till you spent all my _____
No use for you to **cry**
I'm waving you _____
'Cos I'm walking to New Orleans.

I've got no time for **talking**
I've got to keep on _____
New Orleans is my home
That's the reason why I'm going
Yes, I'm walking to New Orleans.

I'm walking to New Orleans.
Yes, I'm walking to New Orleans …

1 Read and complete the spaces.
   Choose words that rhyme with the words in blue.
   Listen and check. ✱1.99

2 Find words or phrases in the song which mean:

| because   going to   isn't that a pity   until   girlfriend   finish |

See **Extension 13** p.172

14 What are you doing?

A What's happening?

Martin Trimble is in his office. It's eleven o'clock at night and his computer isn't working. He's phoning his boss at home.

1 Match the beginnings and endings of these questions.
1 Can I speak   A are you, Tiffany?
2 Can I speak   B she doing?
3 How old   C you doing now, Tiffany?
4 Is there   D to your father, please?
5 What's   E anyone else there?
6 What are   F that noise?
7 What's   G to your mother, then?

2 Listen to the story. (✳ 2.02)

3 Ask and answer.
1 Who's Martin speaking to?
2 What are the parents doing?
3 What's Tiffany doing?
4 What's the helicopter doing?
5 What's happening? Give your ideas.

4 Listen to the end of the conversation. (✳ 2.03)
Pair work. Role-play the conversation from memory.

> **Present continuous**
> *I'm hiding.   She's talking to a policewoman.   They're talking.*
> *I'm not listening.   It isn't working.   They aren't talking.*
> *Is she hiding?   Yes, she is. / No, she isn't.*
> *Are they talking?   Yes, they are. / No, they aren't.*

5 Listen and repeat. (✳ 2.04)
What are you doing?   Who are they talking to?
Where are we going?   What are they doing?

UNIT FOURTEEN

B Thanksgiving dinner

Thanksgiving is the fourth Thursday in November in the USA.
It's Thanksgiving Day at the Fletcher family home in Ohio. The family is home for the holidays, and they're having Thanksgiving dinner.

1 **Look at the picture. Complete the sentences with these words.**

photo baby vegetarian vegetables
wine dinner turkey baseball cap

Bob is serving the .... He's putting slices onto a plate.
Linda isn't sitting, she's standing. She's serving the ....
Brad is holding a glass of ....
Sherry is feeding Mia, the ....
Gary is holding his plate. He's wearing a ....
Mike is taking a ....
Amy is a .... She's giving her turkey to the dog.
Bart is eating his ....

Listen and check. (✱ 2.05)

2 **Write the names next to the seats.**

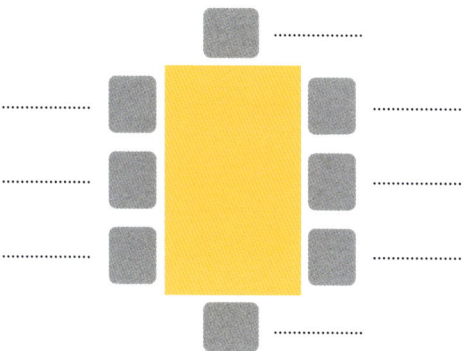

3 **Ask and answer questions with *What* and *Who*.**
   ▶ What's Bob doing?
   ◀ He's serving the turkey.
   ▶ Who's serving the vegetables?
   ◀ Linda's serving the vegetables.

4 **Make sentences.**

Amy's sitting next to Mike.
Amy's sitting between Mike and Bob.
Amy's sitting opposite Brad.

5 **Make sentences about your class.**

I'm sitting next to Anna.
Anna's sitting between me and David.

C Families

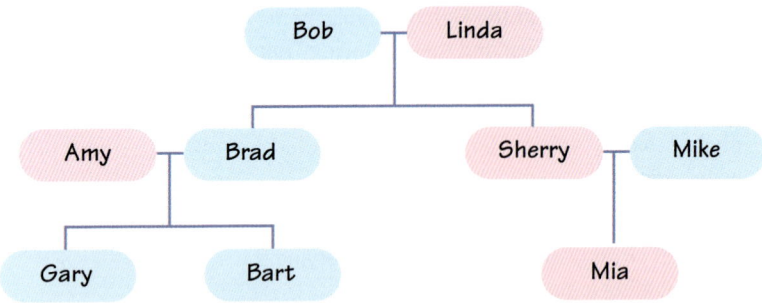

grand +	grandparents, grandfather, grandmother, grandchildren, granddaughter, grandson
+ -in-law	son-in-law, daughter-in-law, mother-in-law, father-in-law, brother-in-law, sister-in-law

1 **Read the sentences about the Fletcher family. Make more sentences.**
Mia is Gary's cousin.
Mike is Bart's uncle.
Mike is Linda's son-in-law.
Bart is Sherry's nephew.
Linda is Bart's grandmother.
Mia is Brad's niece.
Brad is Amy's husband.

2 **Pair work. Student A look at the plan of the seats. Student B look at the family tree. Ask and answer.**
   ▶ Who's Amy?
   ◀ She's Brad's wife. / She's Linda's daughter-in-law. / She's Gary's mother. / She's Mia's aunt.

3 **Talk about your family. What are they doing now?**
My father's at home. He's retired. It's afternoon. I think he's watching TV.
My daughter's at school. I think she's having an English lesson.
My sister-in-law's at work. I think she's working on her computer.

COMMUNICATION

Student A Look at Activity 5 on p.192.
Student B Look at Activity 17 on p.201.

D Film script

```
                'THE FLETCHERS'
           SCENE 52: THE DINING ROOM, DAY

LINDA IS SERVING GARY.

LINDA   Are you OK, hon? You aren't eating your
        turkey.

GARY    Oh, Grandma, I don't like turkey. And Mom
        isn't eating her turkey.

LINDA   Yes, she is, hon.

GARY    No, she isn't. She's giving it to the dog.

AMY     I am not giving it to the dog! It's an
        absolutely delicious dinner, Linda …

BRAD    (LAUGHING) Yes, you are! Come on, Amy, tell
        the truth …

AMY     You're drinking too much, Brad!

BRAD    (SHOUTING) I'm relaxing! We're all having
        fun. What's your problem?

        EVERYBODY STOPS TALKING. MIA STARTS CRYING.

        CUT
```

1 **Listen to the conversation at dinner.** (✱ 2.06)

2 **Ask and answer.**
   1 How old is Gary, do you think?
   2 Is Amy telling the truth?
   3 What's she giving to the dog? Why?
   4 What's Brad drinking?
   5 Is he angry?

3 **Practise the film script. Can you continue the conversation?**

See **Extension 14** p.173

15 I like it

A Compliments

1 **Listen.** (✱ 2.07)
  Who's giving a compliment?
  Who's receiving a compliment?

  Nicola I love your new hairstyle! It really suits you.
  Tasha   Do you think so?
  Nicola Yes, it's great.
  Tasha   Thank you.

2 Listen and practise.

(* 2.08)
Helen Great tie!
Jack Thanks! It's my favourite.

(* 2.09)
Carol I really like your tie.
Tony This one? Oh, it's very old.

(* 2.10)
Marie I love your trainers. They're so cool!
Jessica Thanks, they're new.

(* 2.11)
Al Rosalita? That's a beautiful name.
Rosalita Thank you. It's Spanish. My parents are Mexican.

(* 2.12)
Steve Wow! What a great laptop.
Phil Yeah, it's the latest model.

3 Pronunciation. You can put emphasis in different places.
- ★ I like your tie. <u>Great</u> tie.
- ★★ I <u>really</u> like your tie. Your trainers are <u>so</u> cool.
- ★★★ I <u>love</u> your earrings. I <u>really</u> love your <u>jacket</u>.

Listen and <u>underline</u> the emphasis. (* 2.13)

1 I really like your jeans.
2 This is a lovely meal.
3 That colour really suits you.
4 Is that your dog? He's so sweet.
5 Fabulous dress! You look great.
6 I love your necklace.

B Giving compliments

1 Interview your partner and complete the questionnaire.

Do you like receiving compliments?
- ☐ Yes, I love it. It's wonderful.
- ☐ Yes, I like it. It's nice.
- ☐ No, I don't really like it.
- ☐ No, I hate it. It's embarrassing.

Do you give compliments?
- ☐ Yes, I do.
- ☐ Yes, sometimes.
- ☐ No, I don't.

In your country, what can you give men compliments about?
- ☐ tie
- ☐ jacket
- ☐ glasses
- ☐ eyes
- ☐ aftershave
- ☐ work
- ☐ possessions
- ☐ shirt
- ☐ watch
- ☐ hair
- ☐ weight
- ☐ car
- ☐ name

In your country, what can you give women compliments about?
- ☐ cosmetics
- ☐ eyes
- ☐ possessions
- ☐ jewellery
- ☐ weight
- ☐ name
- ☐ clothes
- ☐ perfume
- ☐ work
- ☐ hair
- ☐ car

2 Discuss your answers to the questionnaire.

3 Read these facts about compliments. Do they surprise you?
- Americans give more compliments than the British or Australians.
- 66% of compliments use only these five adjectives:
  USA: *nice, good, beautiful, pretty, great*
  UK: *nice, good, pretty, lovely, beautiful*
- 66% of all compliments are from women.
- 75% of all compliments are to women.
- People compliment women on clothes and appearance.
- People compliment men on possessions or work.
- In some countries, all personal comments are embarrassing.

4 Go around the class. Give everyone a compliment. Reply to the compliments that you receive.

C Likes and dislikes

Do you like swimming?
Yes, I love swimming. / Yes, I like swimming. / Yes, I do.
No, I don't like swimming. / No, I hate swimming. / No, I don't.

1 Make questions about these things. Think of three more questions to ask. Then go around the class asking the questions.

travelling by air   playing tennis   doing exercise

shopping for clothes   eating in restaurants   playing computer games

dancing   watching football on TV   cooking

meeting people   doing housework   driving

2 Pair work. Talk about people in the class.
   ▶ Does (*Maria*) like travelling by air?
   ◀ Yes, she loves it. / Yes, she does. / No, she doesn't. / No, she hates it.

D *I'd like / I like ...*

1 Listen and circle the words you hear. (* 2.14)
1 (I like / I'd like) coffee, but I don't like tea.
2 (I like / I'd like) a coffee, please.
3 (I love / I'd love) swimming. It's my favourite sport.
4 Thanks, (I love / I'd love) a cold drink.
5 (She likes / She'd like) a chocolate milkshake.
6 (He likes / He'd like) dancing.
7 (Would / Do) you like another drink?
8 (Would / Do) you like travelling by air?

Do you ...? /duː juː/ sounds like 'D'you ...' /djuː/ or /djə/ in conversation. We don't write this contraction.

2 Pronunciation. Listen and repeat. (* 2.15)
Do you like travelling by air?
What do you think?
What do you like doing at weekends?
Do you like Chinese food?

**3 Practise with a partner.
Change the words in *italics*.**
▶ Would you like some *chips*?
◀ No, thanks.
▶ What's the matter?
   Don't you like *chips*?
◀ Yes. I *do*. But I don't
   want any now.

Answer the questions.
Does she like chips?
Would she like some chips now?

4 Group work. Discuss.
What do you like doing in the evenings?
What do you like doing at weekends?
What do you like doing on holiday?

See **Extension 15** p.174

16 Talking about the future

A Arrangements

1 Listen. Adam is busy. What's he doing on these dates? Circle the right date. (✱ 2.16)

Liverpool	8th	11th	12th	15th
bank manager	8th	11th	12th	15th
girlfriend	8th	11th	12th	15th
two appointments	8th	11th	12th	15th

Make sentences.

He's meeting his bank manager on the ...

2 Who says it? Write H (Harry), A (Adam), or C (Chelsea).

1 Let's arrange the next meeting. ....
2 How about Monday the 8th? ....
3 That's good for me. ....
4 What about Thursday the 11th? ....
5 I'm free. ....
6 I can't do Thursday. ....
7 When's good for you? ....
8 Let's meet at ten. ....

Listen again and check.

Future arrangements: present continuous + future time expression
*I'm meeting her tomorrow evening.   I'm not working next week.
Are you seeing the doctor tomorrow?
What are you doing on Monday? I'm going to London.*

Suggestions
Let's meet at ten.   What about Monday?   How about Thursday?

COMMUNICATION

Student A Look at Activity 6 on p.193.
Student B Look at Activity 18 on p.202.
Student C Look at Activity 22 on p.205.

3 Group work. Arrange a time when you can all meet next week.

B The weather

1 Label the compass with these words.

north
south
east
west
south-east
north-west

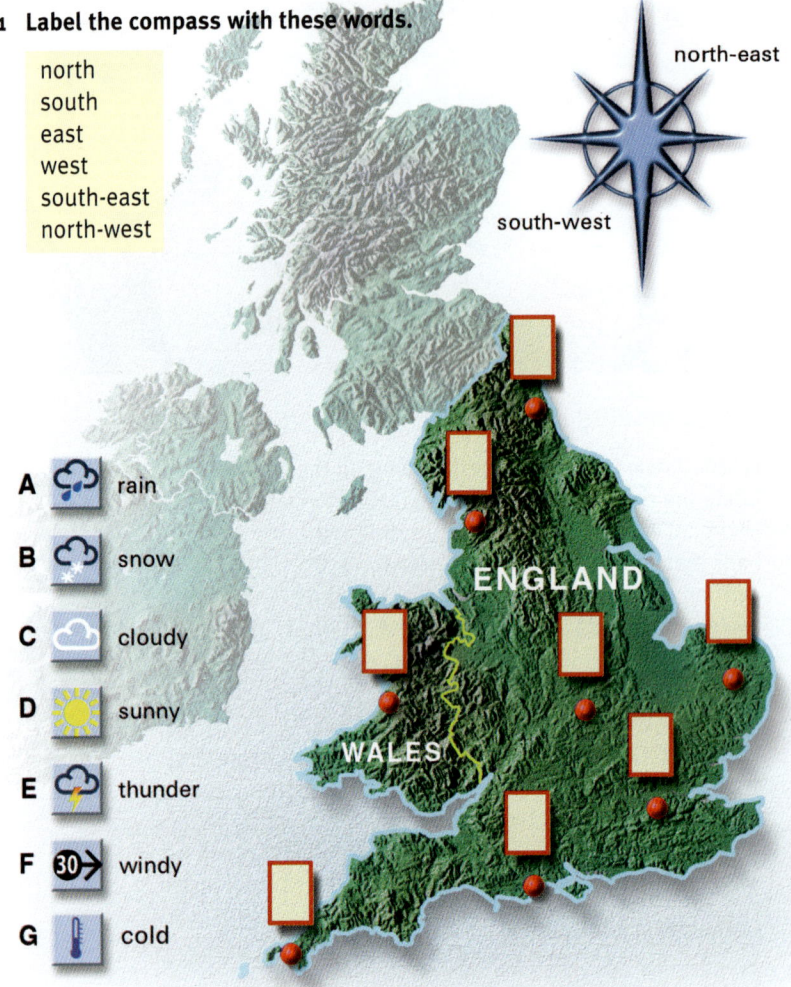

2 Listen to the weather forecast for England and Wales. Put the letters A to G on the map. (* 2.17)

3 Are these sentences true or false?
1 It's going to rain in the south-east.
2 It's going to snow in the north-east.
3 It's going to be a lovely day in the north-west.
4 It's going to rain in Wales.
5 It's going to be cloudy in the south.
6 It's going to thunder in the Midlands.
7 It's going to be windy in the east.
8 It's going to rain in the south-west in the morning.

The future: *be* + *going to* + base form of verb
You can add a time word, but you don't always need to.
It's going to be hot.   It isn't going to snow.   Is it going to rain tomorrow?

4 **Listen to these people. It's March 20th and they're talking about the weather for March 21st. Where are they?**

(✱ 2.18)	First conversation	....
(✱ 2.19)	Second conversation	....
(✱ 2.20)	Third conversation	....
(✱ 2.21)	Fourth conversation	....
(✱ 2.22)	Fifth conversation	....

C Talk about the weather

1 **Months and seasons.
Listen and repeat.** (✱ 2.23)

January	July
February	August
March	September
April	October
May	November
June	December
spring	autumn / fall
summer	winter

2 **Make sentences.**

May is the fifth month.
November is the eleventh month.

3 **What's the weather like in your country?**

It rains in the spring. It's windy in April.
It's warm in May. It's hot in the summer.
It doesn't snow in the winter. It's cold in December.

4 **Talk about the weather forecast for your country.**

It isn't going to rain tomorrow. It's going to be cloudy.
It's going to be hot and sunny next weekend.

Then make conversations.
▶ It's going to (*be hot*) tomorrow.
◀ Let's go to (*the beach*).

D Intentions

1 Match the sentences to the pictures.
1 I'm going to retire next year. ☐
2 I'm going to ask her out. ☐
3 It's Sunday tomorrow. I'm going to get up late. ☐
4 Oh, no! What are we going to do? ☐
5 I'm going to be a ballet dancer when I grow up. ☐
6 What am I going to wear? ☐

Future intentions: *be* + *going to* + base form of verb
You can add a time word, but you don't always need to.
I'm going to buy a new car.   They aren't going to have a holiday.
What are you going to do?   Are you going to be at the party on Saturday?

2 Pronunciation: /tuː/ /tə/.

to is pronounced /tə/ before a consonant sound and /tuː/ before a vowel sound.

I'm going to /tə/ *get up late.*
I'm going to /tuː/ *ask her out.*

too and *two* are always pronounced /tuː/.

Put A /tuː/ or B /tə/ in the boxes.
1. I'm going to ☐ stop smoking.
2. The new cinema's going to ☐ open next week.
3. I'm not going to ☐ have a holiday this year.
4. Are you going to ☐ ask the teacher?
5. I'd like two ☐, please.
6. When is she going to ☐ get a job?
7. He's working, and she's working too ☐.

Listen and check. ✱ 2.24

3 Discuss.
What are you going to do …?
… later today
… tomorrow
… next weekend

4 Talk about your future. Make three predictions.

I'm going to have children.
I'm going to get a good job.
I'm going to study more English.

5
Look at the fortune cookie. Write a silly prediction on a small piece of paper. Put all the predictions from your class in a bag. Each student takes a prediction from the bag and reads it to the class.

You're going to be a millionaire.

See **Extension 16** p.175

17 *Was* and *were*

A We were unlucky.

Jason Dean plays for Newtown United. It's just after the game on Saturday. The final score was Belcaster Rovers 6 Newtown United 0.

Listen and practise. (✱ 2.25)

Manager	Ah, Jason! It wasn't a very good game, eh?
Jason	No, boss. We were a bit unlucky.
Manager	Unlucky! Six times?
Jason	Yeah, well. Very unlucky.
Manager	You were terrible, Jason. Were you tired?
Jason	Tired? No way, boss. I was fine.
Manager	Where were you last night, Jason?
Jason	Me? I was at home.
Manager	Were you alone?
Jason	Alone?
Manager	Who was with you?
Jason	My mum and dad. I was with my parents.
Manager	So you weren't out?
Jason	The night before a game? Oh, no, boss. I was asleep at ten o'clock.
Manager	You aren't telling me the truth, Jason.
Jason	I am, boss.
Manager	OK, Jason. Look at today's newspaper ...

COMMUNICATION

Student A Look at Activity 4 on p.191.
Student B Look at Activity 16 on p.200.

> *Where were you yesterday? Where was he last night?*
> *I was at home. We were with friends.*
> *He wasn't out. They weren't at school.*
> *Were you alone? Yes, I was. / No, we weren't.*

B Where were you yesterday?

1 Pronunciation.

There are two pronunciations of *was* and *were*.
Stressed: was /wɒz/, were /wɜː/   *Yes, she was. Yes, they were.*
Unstressed: was /wəz/, were /wə/   *I was on holiday. We were late.*

You needn't say the unstressed form, but you need to understand it when you are listening.

Listen and write *S* (stressed), or *U* (unstressed). (✱ 2.26)

1 Who was with you? ☐
2 Yes, I was. ☐
3 Was she at home yesterday? ☐
4 I wasn't there last night. ☐
5 No, she wasn't. ☐
6 Yes, they were. ☐
7 Where were you last night? ☐
8 You weren't late. ☐

2 Pair work. Look at the chart. Ask your partner about these times.

yesterday lunchtime   yesterday afternoon   last night at 11 p.m.
last Saturday evening   last Sunday morning

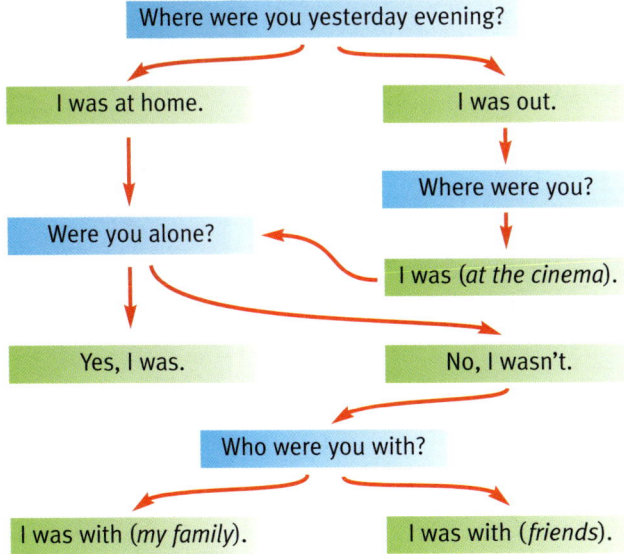

3 Change partners. Ask about your first partner.

Where was (*she*) (*yesterday evening*)?

C Quiz

1 Do the quiz with a partner.

SPORT
The first modern Olympic Games were in 1896. Where were they?
A Paris
B Athens
C London

POPULAR CULTURE
When was the first episode of 'Star Trek'?
A 1966
B 1976
C 1996

NATURAL HISTORY
When were dinosaurs alive?
A about 60 million years ago
B about 6 million years ago
C about 600,000 years ago

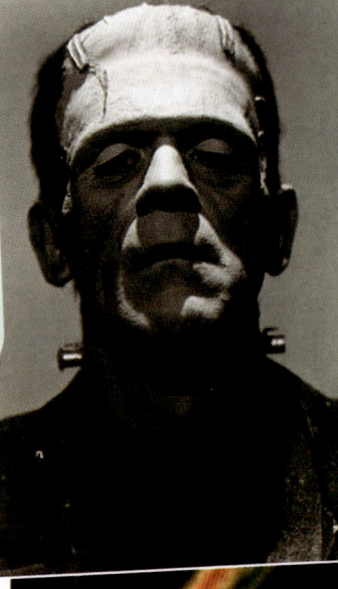

HISTORY
Who was Cleopatra?
A the Queen of Rome
B the Queen of England
C the Queen of Egypt

LITERATURE
Who was the author of 'Frankenstein'?
A Agatha Christie
B Mary Shelley
C Charles Dickens

2 Listen to the quiz show and find the correct answers. (✻ 2.27)

3 Write five more quiz questions with *was* and *were*.
Ask your partner.

UNIT SEVENTEEN

D When were you born?

1 Listen and repeat. (* 2.28)

| 1st | 11th | 21st | 31st | 3rd | 13th | 23rd | 30th |
| 2nd | 12th | 20th | 22nd | 4th | 5th | 12th | 25th |

2 Say these dates aloud.

21/6/02   The twenty first of June, two thousand and two.

5/11/98   24/12/85   16/3/01   30/9/05   28/1/74   15/8/00
12/5/99   20/4/88   22/6/03   31/1/04   23/2/02   24/7/63

Listen and check. (* 2.29)

Prince William

Madonna

3 Complete the sentences with *He* or *She*.
1 .... was born in St Mary's Hospital, London.
2 .... was born on 16th August 1959.
3 .... was born on 21st June 1982.
4 .... was born in Rochester, Michigan.

4 Ask and answer.
1 When was Prince William born?
2 Where was Madonna born?
3 Where were you born?
4 Were you born at home? In a hospital? Somewhere else?
5 When were you born?
6 Where were your parents born?
7 When were your children born?

5 Can you remember? How old were you?
Where was your first home?
What was your favourite toy?
What was the name of your first school?
Who was your first friend?
When was your first English lesson?

See **Extension 17** p.176

18 What did you do?

A Breakfast survey

1 **Name the food items in the pictures.**

2 **Listen and practise.** ✱ 2.30
Nutritionists say that breakfast is the most important meal of the day, but most people don't have a good breakfast. A market researcher is asking people about their breakfasts.

Researcher What do you usually have for breakfast?
Sonja Oh, I have a boiled egg and some toast.
Researcher What about this morning? What did you have?
Sonja I didn't have breakfast this morning.
Researcher Why not?
Sonja I didn't have time. I was late for work.
Researcher Didn't you have anything to drink?
Sonja Yes, I had a cup of coffee. But that was all.

3 **Find the past of *have* and the past of *don't have* in the conversation.**

4 **Listen and complete the table. Find the items in the pictures.**

		Where?	Anything to eat?	Anything to drink?
✱ 2.31	Ken	in a diner		
✱ 2.32	Amanda			
✱ 2.33	Brendan			

5 **Pair work. Ask and answer.**
What did you have for breakfast / lunch / dinner yesterday?
Where did you have breakfast / lunch / dinner yesterday?
Did you have anything to eat between meals?

B Gary and Tina's honeymoon

1 **When Gary and Tina got married, they went to Niagara Falls in Canada for their honeymoon. Match the sentences to the pictures.**

A We had dinner in an expensive restaurant. ☐
B We both got very wet. ☐
C Our hotel room was amazing. ☐
D We bought a lot of souvenirs. ☐
E We went to Niagara Falls by car. ☐
F Gary got food poisoning. ☐
G We saw the Falls from a boat. ☐
H We flew to Toronto. ☐

Listen and check. (✱ 2.34)

2 Underline the past tenses of the verbs in 1.

3 Complete the questions with the correct verbs.
1 Did they .... to Toronto?
2 How did they .... to Niagara Falls?
3 What .... their hotel room like?
4 Did they .... the Falls?
5 Did they both .... wet?
6 Where did they .... dinner?
7 Did he .... food poisoning?
8 Did they .... any souvenirs?

Listen and check. (✱ 2.35)

4 Pair work. Ask and answer the questions in 3.

C The past simple

Questions and negatives
The auxiliary verb changes to the past. The main verb doesn't change.
Present: *Do you have breakfast at home? Yes, I do. / No, I don't.*
           Does she go to work by bus? Yes, she does. / No, she doesn't.

Past: *Did you have breakfast yesterday? Yes, I did. / No, I didn't.*
           Did she go to work by bus?   Yes, she did. / No, she didn't.

Positive
Change the main verb to the past simple.
Present: *I have breakfast at home.*   *She goes to work by bus.*
Past: *I had breakfast at home.*   *She went to work by bus.*

1 Ask and answer.
▶ Did you go anywhere on holiday last year?
◀ Yes, I did. / No, I didn't.

1 Did you fly anywhere last week?
2 Did you buy anything yesterday?
3 Did you come here by car?
4 Did you see a film last night?
5 Did you get any letters yesterday?
6 Did you eat anything before the lesson?
7 Did you drink anything with your breakfast?

You don't need to know the past tenses of the verbs for exercises 1 and 2.

2 Answer with negatives.
▶ Did she go out last night?
◀ No, she didn't go out last night.

1 Did they have lunch in a café yesterday?
2 Did she go on holiday last year?
3 Did we come to school yesterday?
4 Did he know the answers?
5 Did she understand the exercise?
6 Did you do any homework last night?

3 Match the past verbs with the present verbs in 1 and 2.

Past	Present	Past	Present
had	....	flew	....
went	....	saw	....
did	....	got	....
understood	....	drunk	....
came	....	ate	....
bought	....	knew	....

D Questions

Ask and answer questions around the class.

Shopping
go shopping / last weekend?   Did you go shopping last weekend?
What / buy?   What did you buy?
How much?   How much was it?

Shopping
go shopping / last weekend?
What / buy?
How much?

Holidays
have a holiday / last year?
Where / go?
How / go there?

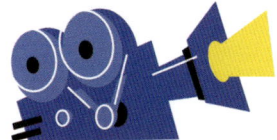

Films
see a film / last month?
Which film / see?
What / it like?

Eating out
eat in a restaurant / last week?
Where / go?
What / have?

Post
get any letters / yesterday?
How many / get?
Who / from?

Going out
go out / last night?
Where / go?
Who / with?

See **Extension 18** p.177

19 What happened?

A A new star

1 **Listen and read the newspaper story and underline the verbs in the past. How many of the verbs end in -ed?** ✱ 2.36

Nineteen-year-old Shaun Clancy is the new member of teen-band Eye Dolls. The band needed a new singer, so they decided to have a competition. Last night the ten finalists sang and danced on TV, and viewers phoned the TV station with their votes.

Shaun was born in Belfast, and moved to Manchester when he was ten years old. He left school at sixteen, and worked in a supermarket. Shaun wanted to be an actor, and studied acting in his free time. He saw the advert for Eye Dolls and travelled to London for the competition. The band listened to 1500 young singers, and selected ten for the TV programme. Shaun came first with over 400,000 votes. 'This is the dream of a lifetime,' said Shaun. The band is recording a new album with Shaun next week, then they are going on tour.

NEW BOY JOINS 'EYE DOLLS'

2 Zoe Hall interviewed Shaun on TV. Complete the interview.

Zoe Wow! Congratulations, Shaun. You were great!
Shaun Thank you, Zoe. I can't believe it.
Zoe So, Shaun, tell us about yourself. Where .... ?
Shaun Belfast, but my parents .... to Manchester later.
Zoe How .... then?
Shaun I was ten.
Zoe .... leave school?
Shaun Three years ago. When I was ....
Zoe Where .... ?
Shaun In a supermarket.
Zoe When did you decide to be a singer?
Shaun I didn't. I .... to be an actor. I .... acting in my free time. But I love singing.
Zoe Are you a fan of Eye Dolls?
Shaun Oh, yeah. This is the .... of a lifetime. They're all really great guys.
Zoe What's going to happen next?
Shaun We're .... a .... next week. Then we're going on tour.
Zoe Well, good luck with your new career, Shaun.
Shaun Thanks, Zoe.

Listen and check. ✱ 2.37

3 Write the past tense of these verbs.

Irregular verbs	Regular verbs		
leave	dance	need	travel ....
sing	decide	phone	want ....
come	listen	select	work ....
see	move	study	

B Twins

1 Pronunciation.

Regular verbs end in *-d* or *-ed* in the past simple. The final *-d* /*-ed* has three different sounds:
/d/ *move – moved* /t/ *work – worked* /ɪd/ *want – wanted*

Put these past verbs in three groups.

danced	phoned	needed	moved	studied	decided
worked	travelled	wanted	selected	listened	

/d/ _____
/t/ _____
/ɪd/ _____

Listen and check. (✷ 2.38)

2 Read the text and underline the past verbs with *-ed* endings. Add the new verbs to the groups in 1: /d/, /t/ or /ɪd/.

Listen and check. (✷ 2.39)

Robin Taylor was born in Birmingham on 27th December 1958. His mother died the same day. Mr and Mrs Taylor adopted him. In 1960, the Taylor family emigrated to Perth in Western Australia. Last year, Robin was in Britain on holiday. He travelled to Birmingham and asked about his family. He discovered that he had a twin brother! Robin phoned a BBC radio programme and told his story. He asked for information about his brother. That afternoon he received a phone call from Perth in Scotland. The next day he went to Scotland and met his twin brother for the first time.

COMMUNICATION

Student A Look at Activity 7 on p.194.
Student B Look at Activity 19 on p.203.

C Life events

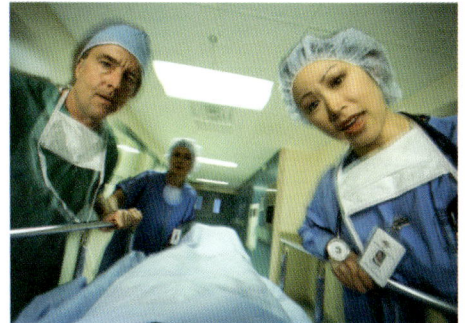

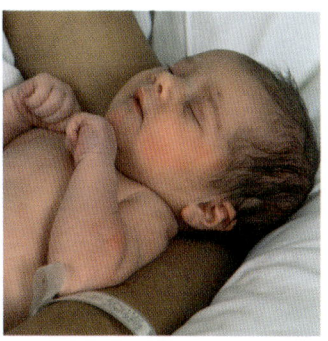

1 Make a list of six important events in your life.

2002: I had an operation.
2003: My uncle died.

Give your partner the list of dates only. Don't tell them what happened.

2 Ask and answer.
- What happened in 2001?
- I started university.

Ask more questions about each event.
- Where did you go to university?
- I went to university in Melbourne.
- What did you study?
- I studied law.
- How old were you then?
- I was nineteen.

3 Write a paragraph about events in your life.

met   got married   passed (an exam)   moved   got divorced
died   was born   started (work)

See **Extension 19** p.178

20 True stories

A The robbers

Page 14

Blind robbery

DETECTIVES in York laughed when they watched videotape from a security camera in July 2001. The video showed two teenage robbers who forgot to cut eyeholes in their masks. The teenagers ran into a newsagent's shop early one morning, and both pulled their woollen hats over their faces. Then one bumped into the other, and they demanded money from a shop wall. The newsagent phoned the police, but they didn't see her. Then they pulled off their masks right in front of the security camera. They only took three packets of cigarettes from the shop. The police arrested them twenty minutes later.

UNIT TWENTY

1. **Listen and read. <u>Underline</u> the regular past verbs.** ✱ 2.40

2. **Put the regular past verbs in three sound groups.**

/d/
/t/
/ɪd/

3. **Find:**
   1. the past tense of *run*
   2. the past tense of *forget*
   3. the past tense of *take*

   Find words in the text which mean:
   4. a shop that sells newspapers
   5. something that covers the face
   6. holes you can look through
   7. requested something very strongly
   8. hit against someone or something by accident

4. **Answer the questions.**
   1. When was the robbery?
   2. What did the robbers forget to do?
   3. When did they run into the shop?
   4. What did they pull over their faces?
   5. What did they demand money from?
   6. Who phoned the police?
   7. Where did they pull off their masks?
   8. What did they take from the shop?
   9. When did the police arrest them?

> **Subject questions**
> *Who* phoned *the police?* *The newsagent* did.
>
> **Object questions**
> *Who* did *the newsagent* phone? *She* phoned *the police*.

5. **Make questions.**
   Someone phoned the police.

   Who phoned the police?

   1. Someone laughed at the videotape.
   2. Someone forgot to cut eyeholes.
   3. Someone demanded money.
   4. Someone took cigarettes from the shop.
   5. Someone arrested them.

   Now answer the questions.

FREE flight

SEVENTEEN-YEAR-OLD Chris Grimes from Essex liked flying his kite in his free time. In March 2000 he got a nasty surprise. He took his kite to the river near his home. Suddenly a strong wind carried the kite high into the air. Chris held onto his kite and it lifted him about ten metres into the air, and straight across the river. In the middle of his journey, he came down in the water, and his trousers fell down. Then he was lifted up again, with his trousers round his ankles. Finally, he landed in the mud on the other side of the river, half a mile away. Luckily he wasn't hurt, and he didn't lose his kite, but he was cold, wet, and very embarrassed.

B The kite

1. **Listen and read.**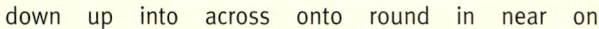

2. **Find the past of these verbs in the text.**
   carry   come   fall   get   hold   land   lift   like   take

3. **Label the diagrams with these words.**

   down   up   into   across   onto   round   in   near   on

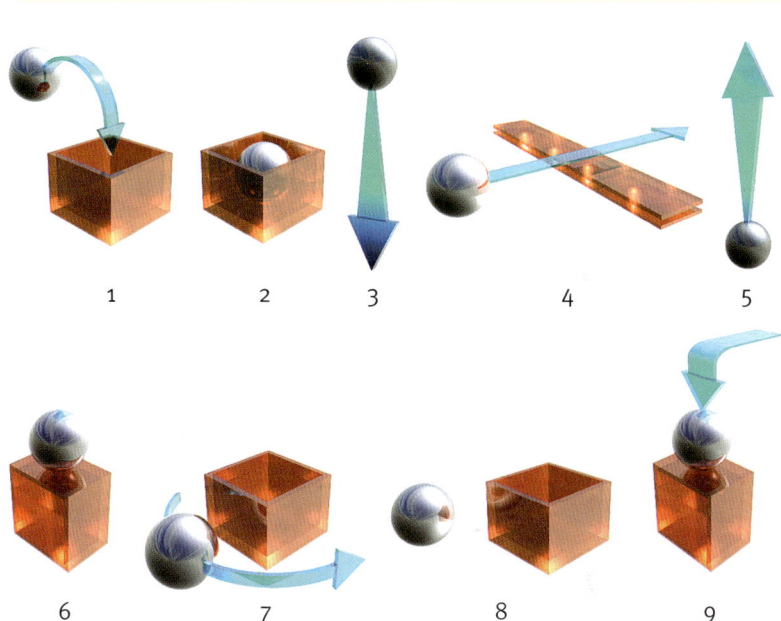

4. **Complete the sentences with words from 3.** (One word is used twice)
   The river was .... Chris's home. A strong wind carried the kite .... the air. Chris held .... the kite. The kite carried him .... the river. He came .... in the water. His trousers fell .... He was lifted .... again, and his trousers were .... his ankles. He landed .... the mud .... the other side of the river.

5. **Complete the sentences with these words.**

   Finally   Suddenly   Luckily

   1. .... a strong wind lifted the kite.
   2. .... he landed in the mud.
   3. .... he was OK.

C The banknote

One in 209 million

Mark Goldsmith was angry when his six-year-old daughter drew on a £5-note. She drew glasses and a moustache on the picture of the Queen. Mark put the note in his pocket. He thought it was useless. The next day he bought some petrol near his home, and paid with the note by mistake. Two weeks later he was 200 miles away in Harrogate, Yorkshire. He bought some food at a supermarket. He gave the cashier a £20-note and got a £5-note in his change. To his surprise, it was the £5-note with his daughter's drawing on it. He brought it home and put it in a picture frame on the wall. This happened in August 2000, when there were 209 million £5-notes in Britain.

1 Listen and read. <u>Underline</u> the past verbs. (✱ 2.42)

2 Are these sentences true or false?
1 She wrote her name on the £5-note.
2 Mark put the note in his wallet.
3 He bought some petrol in Harrogate.
4 He paid with a credit card.
5 Two weeks later he was 200 miles away.
6 He bought some shampoo at a supermarket.
7 He gave the cashier a £10-note.
8 He got a £5-note in his change.
9 He brought it home.
10 He put it in a photo album.

3 Correct the false sentences.
She wrote her name on the £5-note.
No, she didn't. She drew glasses and a moustache on the £5-note.

D Return to Sender

1 The song 'Return to Sender' was a hit for Elvis Presley.
Listen and complete the spaces with the past of these verbs.
One verb is used twice (*2.43)

> write give send come bring drop have put

RETURN TO SENDER
Blackwell / Scott

Return to sender! Return to sender!
I .... a letter to the postman
He .... it in his sack
Bright and early next morning
He .... my letter back.

She .... upon it
'Return to sender, address unknown,
No such number, no such zone'.

We .... a quarrel, a lovers' spat
I write 'I'm sorry'
but my letter keeps coming back.

So when I .... it in the mailbox
I .... it Special D
Bright and early next morning
It .... right back to me.

She .... upon it
'Return to sender, address unknown,
No such person, no such zone'.

This time I'm gonna take it myself
And put it right in her hand
And if it comes back the very next day
Then I'll understand

The writing on it
'Return to sender, address unknown,
No such person, no such zone'.
Return to sender.
Return to sender ...

2 Look at the envelope. Find:
the meaning of 'Special D'   the street number
the zip code (zone)   the city
the apartment number

See **Extension 20** p.179

21 Healthy living

A Good food?

You are what you eat.

An apple a day keeps the doctor away.

More die in the United States of too much food than too little.
J. K. Galbraith

Eat what you like, and let the food fight it out inside of you.
Mark Twain

Eat, drink and be merry for tomorrow we die.

Some people eat to live. Others live to eat.

1 **Read the sayings. Do you agree or disagree?**

2 **Listen. Which sentences are true for you?** (✱ 2.44)
   1 I always put salt on my dinner.
   2 I always put sugar in tea and coffee.
   3 I usually drink two litres of water a day.
   4 I usually eat five portions of fruit or vegetables a day.
   5 I often eat snacks between meals.
   6 I often eat fast-food.
   7 I sometimes eat too much.
   8 I sometimes drink too much alcohol.
   9 I hardly ever eat fried food.
   10 I hardly ever have desserts after meals.
   11 I never eat fresh fruit.
   12 I never drink coffee in the evening.

3 **Put these adverbs of frequency in the table.**

   never   often   sometimes   always   hardly ever   usually   not often

	100% of the time
	most of the time, 75% to 99% of the time
	many times
sometimes	anything from 1% to 50% of the time
	not many times
	very few times, 0.1% of the time
	0% of the time

4 **Pair work. Look at 2. Ask your partner questions.**
   ▶ Do you put salt on your dinner?
   ◀ Yes, always. / Yes, often. / Yes, sometimes.
   or
   No, hardly ever. / No, not often. / No, never.

B Eating habits

1 **Look at these sentences.
Then make a list of things you never eat.
Give a reason.**

| I never eat | beef
pork
shellfish
salad
nuts
chips | because | I don't like it / them.
I'm vegetarian.
of my religion.
I'm allergic to it / them. |

2 **What do you usually drink with meals?**
☐ water ☐ tea
☐ soft drinks (e.g. cola) ☐ milk
☐ beer ☐ wine

Make sentences about different meals.

I usually drink coffee with breakfast.
I usually drink water with lunch.

3 **Make sentences about your eating habits.**

| I | always
usually
often
sometimes
hardly ever
never | eat | cereal
fries
fruit
meat
vegetables
salad
biscuits
dessert | for
with my
after my | breakfast.
lunch.
dinner.
morning break.
afternoon break. |

4 **Doctors say the food items in the table below are good for you. How often do you eat them? Make sentences.**

I	eat	fish vegetables salad fruit	once twice three times four times	a week. a day.
		olive oil white meat	every day.	

5 **Doctors say too much of these things is bad for you. How often do you eat or drink them? Make sentences.**

salt   sugar   red meat   chocolate
coffee   fried food   alcohol

6 **In your opinion, which things are good for you? Which things are bad for you? Discuss.**

7 **Can you find these things in the picture?**

a cherry   a courgette   a pear   a grape   a peach   an artichoke
a raspberry   a melon   garlic   wheat   peas   sweetcorn

C Taking exercise

1 Listen. Find the people in the picture.

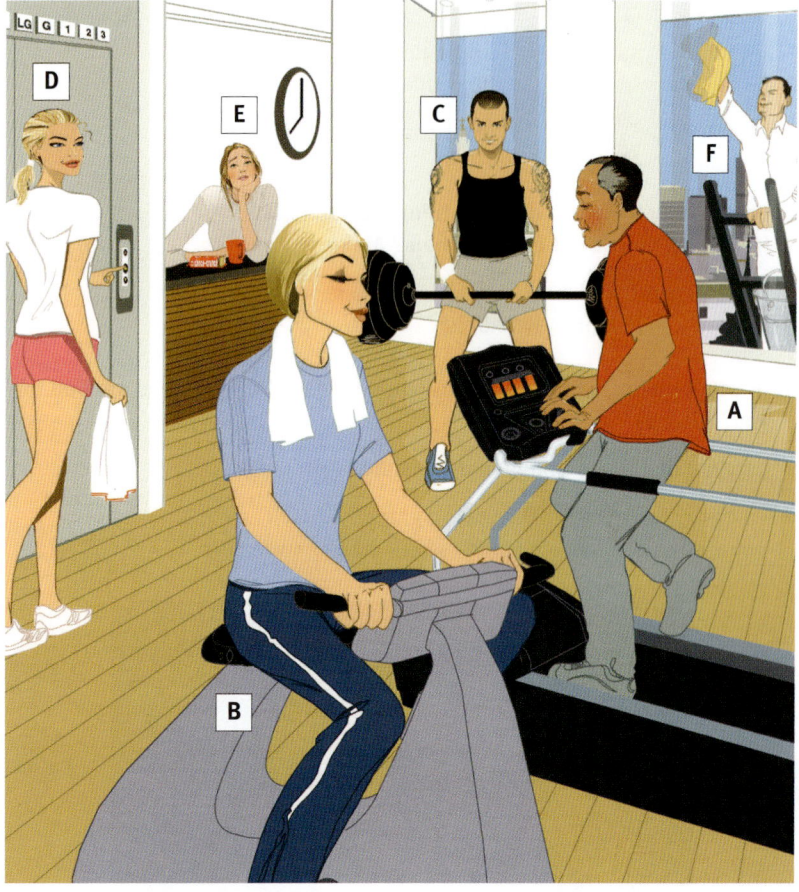

✳ 2.45	✳ 2.46	✳ 2.47	✳ 2.48	✳ 2.49	✳ 2.50

When / What time do you go to bed?
I (**always** / **usually**) go to bed at 11 p.m.

How often do you take exercise?
I take exercise (**once** / **twice** / **three times**) a (**week**).

Do you take exercise?
Yes, I (**often** / **sometimes**) take exercise.
No, I (**don't often** / **hardly ever** / **never**) take exercise.

2 Interview a partner and complete the questionnaire.

HEALTH QUESTIONNAIRE

1 How often do you take exercise?
- ☐ once a week
- ☐ three times a week
- ☐ every day
- ☐ hardly ever
- ☐ never

2 How often do you do these things?
- walk more than one kilometre ....
- play a competitive sport ....
- run or jog ....
- swim ....
- go to a gym ....
- go dancing ....
- do yoga ....
- do martial arts ....
- ride a bicycle ....

3 You've got an appointment with someone on the 3rd floor. Do you …
- ☐ take the lift?
- ☐ walk up the stairs?

4 Do you take vitamin tablets?
- ☐ Yes, every day.
- ☐ Yes, often.
- ☐ No, not often.
- ☐ No, never.

5 At work, do you sit down …
- ☐ all day?
- ☐ nearly all day?
- ☐ sometimes?
- ☐ hardly ever?
- ☐ never?

3 Change partners. Ask about your first partner.

D Everyday habits

1 Complete the sentences with these frequency adverbs. Make the sentences true for you.

| always | usually | often | sometimes | hardly ever | never |

1 I .... sleep eight hours a night.
2 I .... walk to work.
3 I .... get up before 7 a.m.
4 I .... go to bed after midnight.
5 I .... have breakfast in bed.
6 I .... watch TV in the evenings.

2 Pair work. Ask and answer.
1 What time do you usually get up?
2 How often do you watch TV in the evenings?
3 What do you usually do on Sundays?

Now ask more questions about your partner's routines and habits.

3 Pair work. Ask and answer about yesterday. Add more questions.
1 What time did you get up yesterday?
2 Did you watch TV yesterday?
3 Did you do any exercise yesterday?

See **Extension 21** p.180

22 Describing people

Sunday morning   Monday evening   Wednesday morning   Saturday night

A His clothes, her clothes

1 **Pair work. Find these things in the pictures.**

shorts	shirt	skirt	dress	jacket
suit	T-shirt	sweater	top	belt
tie	scarf	headband	hat	socks
shoes	boots	trainers	uniform	tights

2 **Point to the pictures and talk about the clothes.**
   ▶ What's he wearing in this picture?
   ◀ He's wearing dark blue shorts, a blue T-shirt, light blue trainers, and white socks.

| Tuesday evening | Thursday morning | Saturday morning | Saturday night |

3 Describe your clothes. Ask and answer.
What are you wearing today?
What's your teacher wearing today?
Describe another student's clothes.

4 Describe clothes in the past. Ask and answer.
▶ What did your teacher wear last lesson?
◀ She wore a grey skirt, with a light blue blouse, and a blue cardigan.

What did you wear yesterday?
What did your partner wear last lesson?

5 Point to the pictures. Talk about routines.
▶ What does he usually wear on Wednesday mornings?
◀ He usually wears a business suit, with a shirt and tie.

B Casual Fridays

1 Read and listen. (✶ 2.51)

Casual Fridays started in the USA in the computer industry. People wore formal clothes from Monday to Thursday, but informal clothes on Fridays. The idea was popular, and moved to other countries.

It's Friday in the office. He usually wears a suit and tie, but today he's wearing an open-necked shirt. She usually wears a skirt and a jacket, but today she's wearing trousers and a sweater.

2 Ask and answer.
1 What does he usually wear?
2 What's he wearing today?
3 What does she usually wear?
4 What's she wearing today?
5 What do you usually wear?
6 What are you wearing today?

Present continuous
now   *It's happening now / at the moment.*
future plans *I'm meeting him on Monday at 12.30.*

Present simple
general   *I **work** in a bank. I **live** in Boston.*
routines   *I **get up** at 7.30.*
with frequency adverbs   *I **usually drink** tea with meals.*

Non-continuous verbs: *like, love, hate, know, understand, mean*
I know her. NOT *I am knowing her.*

---

3 Choose the correct words.
1 I usually (am going / go) to work by train.
2 They (are doing / do) their homework at the moment.
3 (Do you know / Are you knowing) her name?
4 What (do you do / are you doing) next Friday?
5 How often (do you drink / are you drinking) coffee at work?
6 I (understand / am understanding) this exercise.

C Formal or informal?

Smart casual only
NO JEANS.
NO TRAINERS.

NO shirt?
NO shoes?
NO service

Martley Golf Club
Annual Dinner and Dance

8.30 for 9.00

Gentlemen: dinner jackets, black ties
Ladies: evening dresses

1 Are these things formal or informal in your country?
Write *F* (formal), or *I* (informal). Discuss your answers.

For men
- ties
- dark colours
- open-necked shirts
- short-sleeved shirts
- suits
- bright colours
- trainers
- earrings
- hats

For women
- red lipstick
- light colours
- trousers
- jewellery
- high-heeled shoes
- bare legs
- tights
- short skirts
- gloves

2 Ask and answer.
What do you usually wear at work? Do you wear a uniform?
Would you like to wear different clothes at work? Why? / Why not?
How often do you wear jeans?
Do you wear designer labels?
What clothes are in fashion at the moment?
Are you interested in fashion?
What kind of clothes do you like?

D Appearance

1 How many of these features can you find in the photos?

hair colour	white grey blonde red brown black
hair style	straight wavy curly long short a shaved head
for men	clean-shaven unshaven beard moustache
other	glasses earrings
age	about twenty-five about sixty
nationality	Chinese Russian British American
ethnic group	North European / Caucasian (US) Oriental African-American (US) / Afro-Caribbean (UK) Asian Latin Middle-Eastern Hispanic (US)
general	beautiful (women) attractive (both) handsome (men)
height	tall short medium-height
build	slim average-build well-built overweight

UNIT TWENTY-TWO

2 **Match the sentences to the pictures. Add *He* or *She*.**
..........'s young and beautiful.
..........'s got a long, grey beard.
..........'s African-American.
..........'s got long, black, curly hair.
..........'s wearing glasses.
..........'s got a shaved head.

Change 's to *is* or *has*.

3 **Describe the people.
What does he / she look like?**

4 **Listen to the game
'Famous people'.** (*2.52)
These are the rules:
You can ask 20 questions.
You can only ask 'yes / no'
questions.

Cameron Diaz

Now play the game with a group.
One person thinks of a famous
person. The others ask questions.
Choose one person to count the
number of questions.

See **Extension 22** p.181

23 Have you ever ...?

A Have you ever been there?

1 **Tick (✓) the things you have done.**
Have you ever been to the USA?
Have you ever been to London?
Have you ever been to a circus?
Have you ever been to a rock concert?
Have you ever been to a fortune-teller?
Have you ever been to the top of a high building?

2 **Listen and practise.** (✱ 2.53)
▶ Have you ever been to the USA?
◀ No, I haven't.
▶ Have you ever been to London?
◀ Yes, I have.

Pair work. Look at 1. Ask and answer.

3 **Change partners. Ask and answer about your first partner.** (✱ 2.54)
▶ Has she ever been to a fortune-teller?
◀ Yes, she has.
▶ Has she ever been to the top of a high building?
◀ No, she hasn't.

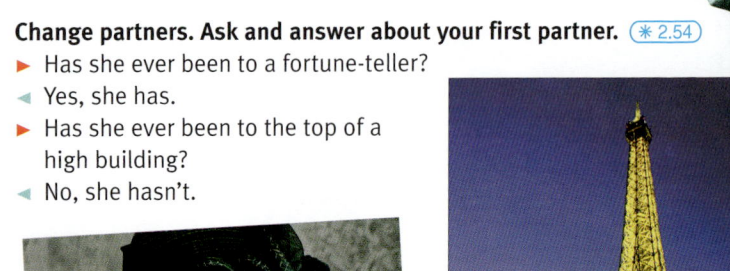

4 Ask and answer about these things.
a country (e.g. Wales)   a city (e.g. Miami)   an opera   a casino
a carnival   a zoo   an international football match

5 Write five negative sentences.
I haven't been to Australia. / I've never been to Australia.
I've never been to a fortune-teller.

6 Talk about yourself.
I've been to a pop concert, but I've never been to a jazz concert.

> **Present perfect: *have* / *has* + past participle**
> ***Have* you *ever been*** to Rome? (= at any time in your life, until now)
> Yes, I have. / No, I haven't.
> **I've been** to Rome.
> I **haven't been** to the Vatican. **I've never been** to the Vatican.
> ***Has*** she ***ever been*** to a fortune-teller?
> Yes, she has. / No, she hasn't.
> He**'s been** to a zoo, but he **hasn't been** to a circus.

B A seven-day tour

1 **Listen to the phone conversation. Tick (✓) the places they've been to.** (✱ 2.55)

2 **Answer the questions.**
Which day is it?
Where have they been?
Where are they going to go?

3 **Ask and answer.** (✱ 2.56)
▶ Have they been to Long Beach yet?
◀ Yes, they have.
▶ When did they go there?
◀ They went on Tuesday.

(✱ 2.57)
▶ Have they been to Sea World yet?
◀ No, they haven't.
▶ When are they going there?
◀ They're going there on Saturday.

> Use **ever** with questions and negatives. **ever** comes before the main verb.
>
> Use **never** with negatives. **never** comes before the main verb.
>
> Use **yet** with questions and negatives. **yet** comes at the end of the sentence.

4 **Complete the sentences with *ever*, *never*, or *yet*.**
1 Have they .... been to Africa?
2 Has he been to the shops .... ?
3 She hasn't been to the USA ....
4 I've .... seen an Australian film.

COMMUNICATION
Student A Look at Activity 10 on p.196.
Student B Look at Activity 21 on p.204.

Long Beach

Disneyland ®

Palm Springs

Itinerary: Seven Days in Southern California

- **Sunday** Arrive in Los Angeles. Transfer to hotel
- **Monday** Universal Studios®, Hollywood
- **Tuesday** Long Beach
- **Wednesday** Disneyland®
- **Thursday** Palm Springs
- **Friday** Joshua Tree National Monument
- **Saturday** San Diego – Sea World®
- **Sunday** Shopping in San Diego. Transfer to airport

Sea World ®

Joshua Tree National Monument

Universal Studios ®

C When did you go there?

Use the past simple to talk about when things happened.
*Have you ever **been** to a zoo? Yes, I have.*
*When **did** you **go**? (I **went** to a zoo) about six months ago.*

1 **Listen and follow the conversation.** (✳ 2.58)
   Make more conversations. Begin *Have you ever been to …?*

   a fortune-teller   a theme park   a dancing class
   an opera   a football match

2 **Complete the second questions.**

First question	Answer	Second question
Have you ever seen a horror film?	Yes, I have.	What did you see?
Have you ever seen a famous painting?		Which one …………?
Have you ever seen an eclipse?		When …………?
Have you ever seen a UFO?		Where …………?
Have you ever seen a famous person in the street?		Who …………?

Now ask your partner the questions. Where have you seen these things?

See **Extension 23** p.182

24 What have you done?

Have you ever bought a souvenir?
What did you buy? Where?

Have you ever met a famous person?
Who did you meet? When?

Have you ever eaten oysters?
Did you like them?
How many did you eat?

Have you ever won a competition?
What did you win?

Have you ever flown in a small plane?
Have you ever flown in a large plane?
Where did you fly to?

Have you ever found money in the
street? How much did you find?
What did you do with it?

A Have you done that?

1 **Listen and repeat the questions.** ✱ 2.59

2 **Ask your partner the questions.**

B *been* and *gone*

> **been** is the past participle of the verb **be**.
> *Have you ever **been** on TV? Yes, I have. I was on TV three years ago.*
>
> BUT we sometimes use **been** like a past participle of **go**.
> *Have you ever **been** to Portugal? Yes, I have. I went there last year.*
>
> **gone** is the past participle of the verb **go**.
> *Is Mrs Smith here? No, she isn't. She's **gone** to the bank.*
>
> **been** = here now
> **gone** = not here now

1 Read the conversations. Complete with *been* or *gone*.

2 Listen and check. Practise the conversations.

(✴ 2.60)

Frank Have you .... to the cash machine?
Dawn Yes, I have. I went at lunchtime.
Frank Good. Can you lend me some money?
Dawn Sure. How much?

(✴ 2.61)

Kelly I can't find my mobile phone. Have you seen it?
Dawn No, I haven't.
Kelly It was in my bag this morning, and now it's .... !
Dawn I'm sorry, I haven't seen it.

(✴ 2.62)

Tom Hi, is Kelly in?
Dawn No, sorry. She's .... to lunch.
Tom Oh. Is Frank there?
Dawn No, he's .... with her.

(✴ 2.63)

Dawn You're late.
Anna I know, sorry.
Dawn Where have you .... ?
Anna I've just .... to the supermarket. The queues were terrible.

C Video games

1 **Listen and complete.** (✱ 2.64-66)

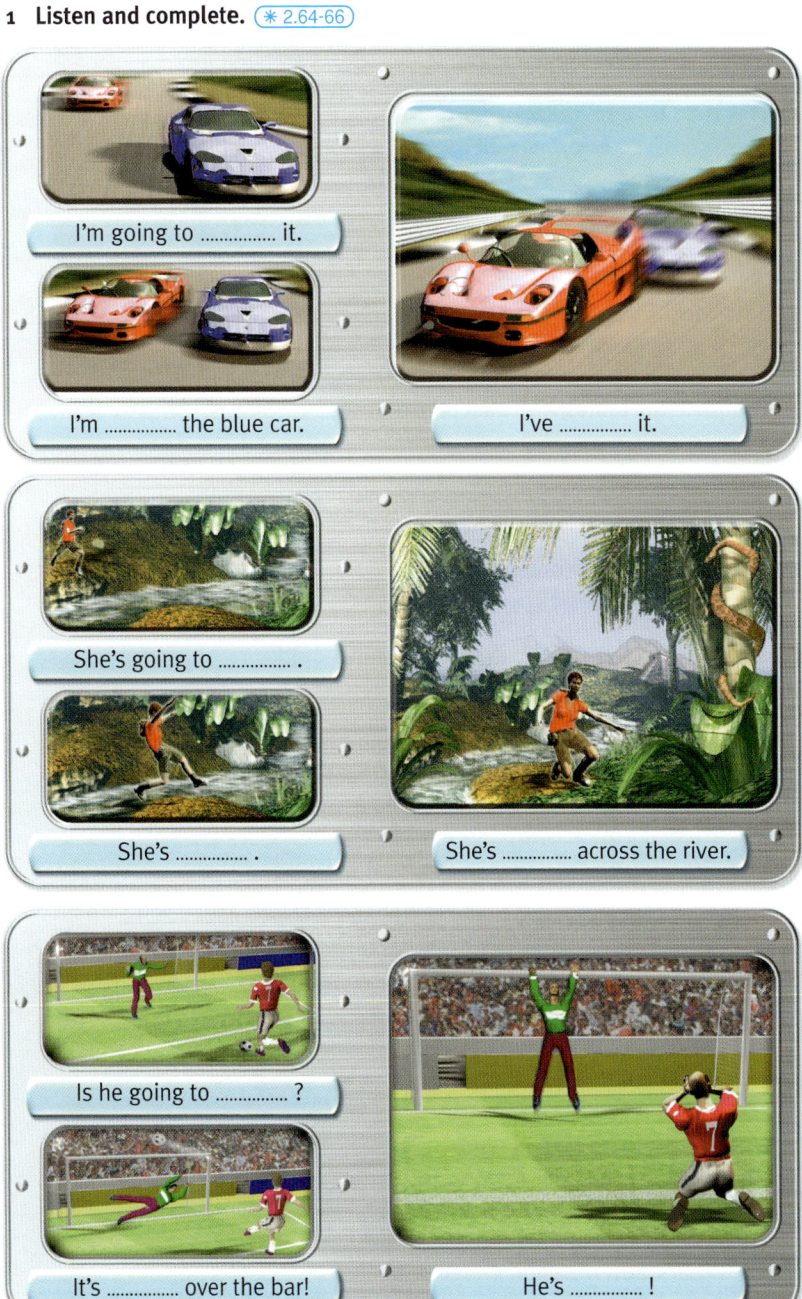

I'm going to .... it.

I'm .... the blue car.

I've .... it.

She's going to ....

She's ....

She's .... across the river.

Is he going to .... ?

It's .... over the bar!

He's .... !

2 **Look at 's above. Does it mean *is* or *has*?**

D Regular and irregular

1 Read the postcard.

Dear _____
This is to let you know that we …
☐ have arrived safe and well.
☐ have arrived.
☐ haven't arrived yet.
☐ have arrived in the wrong place.
☐ have arrived, but our luggage hasn't.
Best wishes from _____

2 Complete the tables with past participles.

Infinitive	be	go	see	buy	meet	eat
Past simple	was/were	went	saw	bought	met	ate
Past participle	been					

Infinitive	win	fly	find	do	jump	pass
Past simple	won	flew	found	did	jumped	passed
Past participle						

How many of the past participles are the same as the past simple?
How many of the past participles are different from the past simple?

Regular verbs: The past participles are the same as the past simple.
*I **passed** an exam last year. I've just **passed** another exam.*

Irregular verbs: Sometimes the past participle is different.
go – went – gone   fly – flew – flown

Sometimes the past participle is the same as the past simple.
buy – bought – bought   have – had – had
When you learn new verbs, try to note all three forms.
do – did – done

3 Pronunciation. Listen and repeat. (✱ 2.67)

/n/	go**n**e bee**n** see**n** do**n**e flow**n** eate**n** wo**n**
/t/	passe**d** jumpe**d** misse**d** watche**d** bough**t** me**t**
/d/	ha**d** arrive**d** phone**d** receive**d**
/ɪd/	want**ed** land**ed** need**ed**

Underline the regular verbs.

E What have you done today?

1. **Ask questions. Find someone in your class who has done these things today. Think of something for the last box.**
   - ► Have you listened to the radio today?
   - ◄ Yes, I have. / No, I haven't.

   Make notes about their answers.

listened to the radio

watched television

bought a newspaper

washed their hair

eaten chocolate

had a shower

kissed someone

received a letter

....

2. **Pair work. Discuss the results with a partner.**
   - ► Has anyone eaten chocolate today?
   - ◄ Yes, Paul has.

See **Extension 24** p.183

25 I'll do it ...

A I'll do it later.

1 **Listen and practise.** (✱ 2.68)

> *will*
>
> **'ll** = will **won't** = will not
>
> **Requests**
> **Will** you help me with my maths? I**'ll** have a coffee, please.
>
> **Deciding**
> You decide either I**'ll** do it. or I **won't** do it. I**'ll** answer the phone.
>
> **Agreeing to do something / Promising**
> This is usually a positive reply to someone. OK, I**'ll** do it. / Yes, I **will**.
>
> **Refusing**
> This is a negative reply. Sorry, I **won't** do that. / No, I **won't**.

2 **Read the story.**
Find two more examples of requests.
Find one example of refusing.
Find four examples of agreeing to do something / promising.

B Requests

1 What are they saying in the cartoons? Choose from the box.

Get me a coffee.
A coffee, please.
I'll have a coffee.
Will you get me a coffee?
Can I have a coffee?
Can you get me a coffee?
Could I have a coffee?
I'd like a coffee.
Would you get me a coffee?

You can add **please** to any of these requests.

In English the sound of your voice is more important than the words you use. You can say any of these requests in a polite way, a neutral way, or as a command.

could is a polite form of **can**. **would** is a polite form of **will**.
In an informal situation (talking to a friend), we often don't use polite forms.

2 Listen. Do these requests sound polite (*P*), neutral (*N*) or like a command (*C*)? Write P, N, or C in the boxes. Put ? if you don't know. ✱ 2.69
1 ☐ John, open the window, it's hot in here.
2 ☐ Would you please be quiet?
3 ☐ Will you get me that magazine? Thank you.
4 ☐ Will you help me with this word? I don't understand it.
5 ☐ I'll have two hot dogs with ketchup.
6 ☐ Can I have some milk, please?
7 ☐ Oh, excuse me. Would you close the window? I'm cold.
8 ☐ Hi. Tea, please.
9 ☐ Could I have a glass of water?

Now try and say each request in three different ways.

C No, Sir Jasper!

No, Sir Jasper!
A melodrama in three acts
by Quentin Openshawe

CAST
SIR JASPER – a wicked landlord
AGATHA MEEK – a young girl
MR MEEK – Agatha's old father
MRS SPRY – an amateur detective
HECTOR – Agatha's fiancé

1 **Imagine. Your class is producing a play.
You need people to do these jobs:**

Five actors
Someone to do the lights
Someone to find the costumes
Someone to paint the scenery
Someone to play the music
Someone to make the tea and coffee
A director
Someone to do the make-up
Someone to make the scenery
Someone to sell the tickets
Someone to do the sound effects

Someone to prompt (to hold the book and correct the actors' mistakes)

Work in groups. Offer to do the jobs.

> I'll be Sir Jasper!   I'll make the tea.   I'll do the make-up.

2 **If you can't decide, choose the director first.
Then the director chooses the jobs.**

Anna, will you be Mrs Spry?   Paul, will you do the lights?

D Play script

'No, SIR JASPER!'

ACT 1. SCENE 2: AGATHA'S COTTAGE, DAY
SIR JASPER HAS JUST ARRIVED AT THE COTTAGE

SIR JASPER   (HE KNEELS) Agatha, will you marry me?
AGATHA   Oh, Sir Jasper, I can't! I love another man.
SIR JASPER   (HE STANDS UP) You forget, my dear. Your father owes me a lot of money.
AGATHA   My father? He's old and sick. We'll pay you soon, I promise.
SIR JASPER   I want the money today!
AGATHA   We haven't got any money! But we'll get it. I'll sell my jewellery!
SIR JASPER   Pay me now, or I'll throw you out on the streets!
AGATHA   Oh, no! Please! Don't!!
SIR JASPER   Then you will marry me, my dear!
AGATHA   Oh, no, I won't!
SIR JASPER   Oh, yes, you will.
AGATHA   Oh, no, I won't!
SIR JASPER   Oh, yes, you will.
AGATHA   Oh, no, I won't!
SIR JASPER   I'll ask you again. Will you marry me, or won't you?
AGATHA   I'll never marry you! Go away, you wicked, wicked man!

1 **Listen to the play.** ✱ 2.70
2 **Practise the play script.**

See **Extension 25** p.184

26 Predictions

A A few questions ...

1 **Listen and read.** (✶ 2.71)
   There has been a census in Britain every ten years since 1801. This advert was in newspapers and magazines. The Government wanted people to complete their census forms. It needs information, so it can make plans for the future about schools, hospitals, and transport. The baby girl in the photo was nine months old.

2 **Ask and answer.**
   When was the last census in Britain?
   Why does the Government need information?
   Does your country have censuses?
   Have you ever completed a census form?
   Can you remember what kind of questions were on it?

3 **Listen and repeat the questions.** (✶ 2.72)
   What questions have you got about your future?
   Will I pass my exams?

B We'll be late.

1 **Read the conversation. Predict which words complete the spaces. Both alternatives are possible.**

2 **Listen and check. Practise the conversations.**

(✱ 2.73)

Ram Are you (packed / ready)?
Leela Yes, I think so. All the bags are (packed / ready).
Ram Have you closed the (doors / windows)?
Leela Yes, of course I have. Have you called the taxi?
Ram Yes. It'll be here (soon / in a minute).

(✱ 2.74)

Ram Where's the taxi? It ('s late / isn't here).
Leela It'll be here (soon / in a minute).
Ram We'll be late for the flight.
Leela No, we won't. There's (plenty / lots) of time.
Ram We'll miss the plane.
Leela Don't worry. It'll be (all right / OK).

(✱ 2.75)

Ram Heathrow Airport, please.
Driver (All right / OK).
Ram How long will it take?
Driver About half an hour. It depends on the (weather / traffic).
Ram Good. We'll be there (early / on time).

Things we think or believe about the future
It**'ll** happen. She**'ll** be late for work. I think I**'ll** go to London on Sunday.
It **won't** happen. He **won't** be on time. They **won't** be at the party.

C Pronunciation

1 **Listen and repeat.** (✱ 2.76)
ll /l/   I'll /aɪl/   you'll /juːl/   he'll /hiːl/   she'll /ʃiːl/   we'll /wiːl/   they'll /ðeɪl/
We'll be late.   She'll be here soon.   They'll be early.

it'll /ɪtl/   what'll /wɒtl/
It'll be here.   What'll you do?

2 **The contraction 'll is sometimes difficult to hear.
Listen and circle the words you hear.** (✱ 2.77)
1 (I / I'll) leave for the airport at seven thirty.
2 (They / They'll) arrive at ten fifteen.
3 (We / We'll) never get there on time.
4 (You / You'll) finish soon.
5 (They / They'll) come home on Saturday.

Was that difficult? Listen again to the sentences in situations. (✱ 2.78)

Timetable future
When we're talking about timetables we often use the present simple.
The bus **leaves** at ten.   Flight BA294 **arrives** at 21.45.

3 **Listen and practise.** (✱ 2.79)
Ram   We haven't moved for forty-five minutes!
Driver Sorry. It usually takes half an hour.
Ram   We'll get out and walk! It'll be quicker.

D Song

1 **Listen.** (✱ 2.80)

Leaving on a Jet Plane
JOHN DENVER

All my bags are packed, I'm ready to go
I'm standing here outside your door
I hate to wake you up to say goodbye.
But the dawn is breaking, it's early morn
The taxi's waiting, he's blowing his horn
Already I'm so lonesome I could cry.
CHORUS
So kiss me and smile for me
Tell me that you'll wait for me
Hold me like you'll never let me go.
I'm leaving on a jet plane
I don't know when I'll be back again
Oh, babe, I hate to go.

There's so many times I've let you down
So many times I've played around
I tell you now, they don't mean a thing.
Every place I go, I think of you
Every song I sing, I sing for you
When I come back, I'll wear your wedding ring.
CHORUS

Now the time has come to leave you
One more time, let me kiss you
Then close your eyes, I'll be on my way.
Dream about the days to come
When I won't have to leave alone
About the time I won't have to say ...
CHORUS

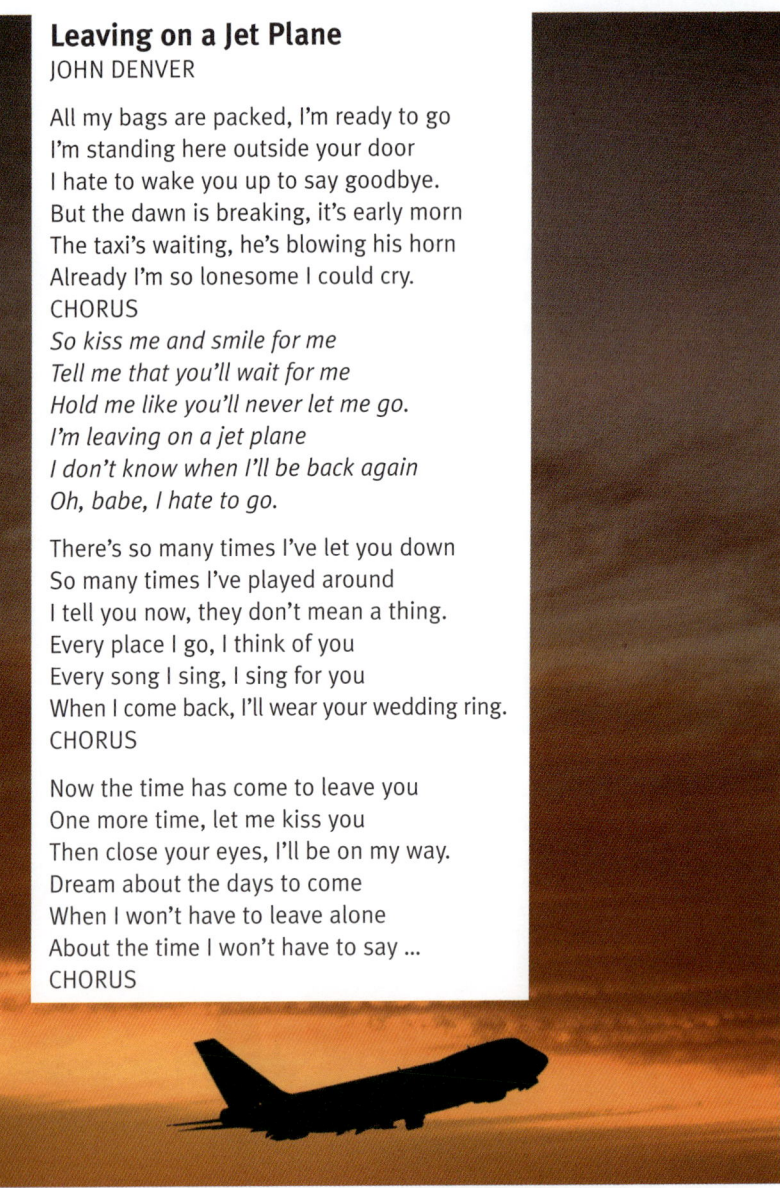

2 **Find words in the song that rhyme with these words.**

| goodbye | morn | plane | down | thing | way |

Listen and sing.

See **Extension 26** p.185

27 Comparisons

A Pub quiz

1 Pub quizzes are popular in England.
  Cover the questions and listen. (✱ 2.81)

2 Look at the questions, and choose the correct words.
  Can you remember the answers? Listen again and check.

QUESTIONS

1 Is the planet Venus (biggest / bigger) than the Earth, or (smaller / smallest) than the Earth?
2 Which is the (higher / highest) mountain in the world?
3 Which is the (more / most) dangerous insect in the world?
4 Are dogs (more / most) popular than cats as pets in Britain?
5 Which is the (older / oldest) university in North America?

B Superlatives

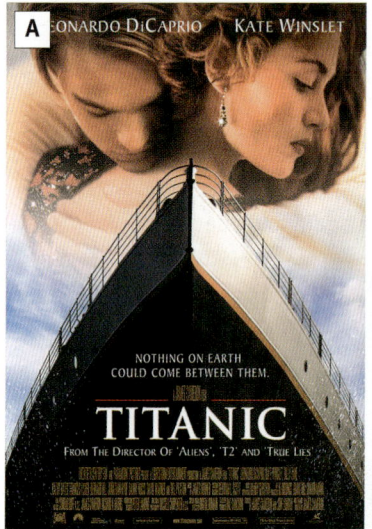

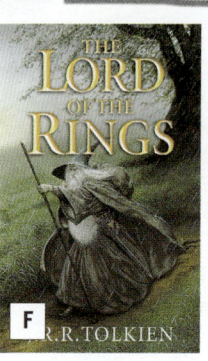

1 **Match to the pictures.**
   The greatest rock album of all time. ....
   The fastest-selling record ever. ....
   The best book of the 20th century. ....
   The largest planet in our solar system. ....
   The worst natural disaster of the 20th century. ....
   The most popular film of the 20th century. ....
   The most expensive film of the 20th century. ....
   The most successful international football team. ....

2 Which ones are facts and which ones are opinions?
  Do you agree with the opinions?

COMMUNICATION

Student A Look at Activity 8 on p.195 for more information.
Other students Ask Student A about the facts.

UNIT TWENTY-SEVEN

Superlative form of short adjectives
*young – the young**est** good – the **best** bad – the **worst***

Superlative form of long adjectives
*expensive – the **most expensive** popular – the **most popular***

We use superlatives for facts and opinions.
*Everest is the **highest** mountain in the world.* (fact)
*She's the **best** student in the class.* (opinion)
*It was the **most popular** film of the year.*

3 **Make your own list.**
The best film of last year was ....
The best TV programme of last year was ....
The worst TV programme of last year was ....
The greatest album of all time is ....
The best film of all time is ....
The most popular film in my country is ....
The most successful football team in my country is ....
The worst disaster of last year was ....
The greatest writer in my language is / was ....
The most important book of all time was ....
The most famous person from my country is / was ....

Compare your list with your partner's list.

C Comparatives

Comparative form of short adjectives
young – **younger than**   good – **better than**   bad – **worse than**

Comparative form of long adjectives
expensive – **more expensive than**   popular – **more popular than**

He's **older than** me.   She's **younger than** him.
This one's **more expensive than** that one.
It was **more expensive than** all the other films of the year.

1 **Find someone in your class who ...**
   ... is taller than you.
   ... is older than you.
   ... has got a more expensive watch than you.
   ... is shorter than you.
   ... has got longer hair than you.
   ... has got smaller feet than you.
   ... lives nearer to the school than you.

2 **Make sentences.**

   Paul's got longer hair than me.
   I've got the smallest feet in the class.

Planet of the Apes (1967)

E.T. the Extra Terrestrial (1982 and 2002)

D Visions of the future

Optimist: The world will be a better place than now …
Pessimist: The world will be a worse place than now …

1 Listen to these sentences about the future. Are they optimistic, pessimistic, or neutral? Write *O* (optimistic), *P* (pessimistic), or *N* (neutral) in the boxes. (✱ 2.82)

☐ There will be dinosaurs in zoos.
☐ The world will be wetter.
☐ The world will be drier.
☐ The world will be hotter.
☐ The world will be colder.
☐ Sea levels will be higher.
☐ People will live longer.
☐ Computers will be smaller.
☐ Electronic pets will be popular.

☐ Robots will do most of the work.
☐ More people will be hungry.
☐ All food will be genetically modified.
☐ Aliens will visit the Earth.
☐ There will be more wars.
☐ There will be more people.
☐ Scientists will clone humans.

---

more, most
Most families in Britain have got a TV.   She's busy **most** of the time.
I've bought some **more** books.   I'd like **more** tea, please.
There are seats for three **more** people.

---

2 Discuss the ideas in 1. Use this language:
I think (*there'll be more wars*).
I don't think (*more people will be hungry*).
I agree. / I disagree.

The Terminator series (1984 to 2003)

The Fifth Element (1997)

See **Extension 27** p.186

28 Best friends

A Reading

1 **Before you read. Ask and answer.**

- Which of these things have you read this week?
  ☐ a letter
  ☐ a magazine
  ☐ a newspaper
  ☐ a novel
  ☐ a short story
  ☐ a textbook
  ☐ a cartoon story
  ☐ a dictionary

- Did you read any of them in English?

- How often do you read novels or short stories?

- What kind of stories do you like reading?
  ☐ true stories
  ☐ cartoons
  ☐ funny stories
  ☐ science-fiction
  ☐ romances

2 **Read the story. Don't stop for words you don't know, but highlight them.**
You can look in a dictionary after you've done the exercises in B.

Best friends

PART ONE (✱ 2.83)

A hot tear fell down Zara's cheek. She kissed the children and hugged them at the school door. Thursday was school day, and she always hated it. She missed them so much when they were at school. Most of the time, Zara taught Tommy and Jenny at home with the InterLink. But Thursday was 'social day', when children spent the day at school with other children. Weekends were the loneliest time for her. Then, her employers, Mr and Mrs Cutler, stayed at home, and spent time with their children. Zara always had more housework at weekends. There was washing, and cleaning, and working in the small garden on top of the house.

PART TWO (✱ 2.84)

She walked from the school to the express elevator, and went down seventy-two floors to the shopping mall. On Thursdays she always had coffee with Elektra. They usually met at the school door, but not today. Perhaps Elektra was already in the coffee shop. Elektra was her best friend. People often thought they were sisters, because they looked so similar. She waited in the coffee shop for two hours. She watched the news on her wrist TV. The news was bad again ... another spaceship crash on the Moon. Two hundred and fifty tourists were dead. She felt sad. There were fifty children on the spaceship. Bad news about children, about any children, made her cry. The hot tears fell again.

PART THREE (✻ 2.85)

At 14.00 she took the elevator upstairs to the school. The teacher called to her, 'Zara, can I speak to you for a moment?'

Zara walked obediently into the office.

'Sit down,' said the teacher. 'I'm sorry. I've got some terrible news for you.'

Zara's heart beat loudly. 'Not Mr and Mrs Cutler?'

'No, not them. It's Elektra. She's had an accident. Her fly-car crashed on the way to school ...'

'How are the children?' Zara said immediately. She loved those children, just like she loved Tommy and Jenny.

'They're OK, but I'm afraid Elektra isn't. She rescued both the children after the crash ... but ... well, she's dead.'

The tears again. Always those hot tears. 'She was my best friend,' she said quietly.

The teacher looked surprised. 'Yes, but ... well, surely you knew? Elektra was a child-care robot. I'm very sorry.'

PART FOUR (✻ 2.86)

Zara closed the door to her tiny room. Of course, a robot. Poor Elektra. Her employers weren't nice and friendly like Mr and Mrs Cutler. She worked seven days a week, eighteen hours a day. Of course, Zara worked long hours too. And she never had holidays. Zara sat down on her narrow bed. What a stupid thought, but ... Zara picked up a pair of scissors, and looked down at her arm. She held her breath, stabbed the scissors into her arm, and made a small cut. Just two or three centimetres, but it was enough. There, in the cut, she saw the electric wires and microprocessors.

3 Questions.
1 When did you guess the truth about Zara?
After the first paragraph? In the middle? At the end?
2 What kind of story is it?
3 What year is it? Guess.

4 Listen to the story. (✻ 2.83 – 2.86)

B Comprehension

Pair work. For these exercises, Student A look at the story. Student B ask the questions.

1 **Part one. Are these statements true or false?**
   1 Zara is Tommy and Jenny's mother.
   2 Zara was always lonely when she wasn't with the children.
   3 Zara had more housework on weekdays.
   4 The children went to school once a week.

2 **Part two. Ask and answer.**
   1 What did Tommy and Jenny do every Thursday?
   2 Was Elektra in the coffee shop?
   3 Did Zara and Elektra look different or did they look similar?
   4 Were they sisters?
   5 How long did Zara wait?
   6 How many children were on the spaceship?

3 **Part three. Correct the information.**
   1 Mr and Mrs Cutler had an accident.
   2 The fly-car crashed on its way back from school.
   3 The children rescued Elektra.
   4 Zara knew that Elektra was a robot.

4 **Find these words in part three of the story.**

   obediently   loudly   immediately   quietly

   They're adverbs. Do they come before or after the verb?

5 **Part four. From memory, complete these sentences from the story.**
   1 Zara closed the door to her .... room.
   2 Her employers weren't .... and .... like Mr and Mrs Cutler.
   3 Zara sat down on her .... bed.
   4 Zara picked up a pair of .... , and looked down at her ....
   5 There, in the .... , she saw the .... wires and microprocessors.

   Which of these pictures shows a pair of scissors?

6 **Discuss.**
   Does Zara have feelings?
   Do child-care robots look like people?
   Is child-care an important job?
   Will robots do this job in the future?
   Did Zara think she was a person?

C Word study

1 Which words can follow these verbs? Put a cross (✗) by the wrong word.

met	☐ on Thursdays	☐ in the coffee shop	☐ her	☐ time	
spent	☐ time	☐ money	☐ employers	☐ the day	☐ dollars
looked	☐ the same	☐ similar	☐ television	☐ different	
	☐ surprised	☐ down			
felt	☐ sad	☐ bad news	☐ tired	☐ unhappy	☐ worse

2 Find one example in each group which is not in the story.

Most of the	time	she taught the children at home.
Weekends were the loneliest	time	for her.
She waited a long	time	for Elektra in the coffee shop.
They stayed at home and spent	time	with their children.

She watched the	news	on her wrist TV.
The	news	was bad again.
I've got some terrible	news	for you.
The	news	about Elektra made her cry.

3 Find the past tense of these irregular verbs in the story.

beat fall feel hold know make meet
say sit spend take teach think

Underline the past tense of regular verbs in the story.

4 Complete the sentences with these words.

too again another other similar

1 England and Germany both wear white.
   Their football shirts look ....
2 After her husband died, she didn't get married ....
3 Would you like .... drink?
4 Anna's got brown hair and Sarah's got brown hair ....
5 On her first day, she met the .... students in the class.

D Make a story

Choose a word for each of these categories.
1 a woman's first name (e.g. *Anna*)
2 a holiday destination (e.g. *Florida*)
3 a place with food or drink (e.g. *bar*)
4 a man's name (e.g. *John*)
5 a hair colour (e.g. *blonde*)
6 a geographical location (e.g. *river*)
7 a building (e.g. *bank*)
8 a length of time (e.g. *10 minutes*)
9 a feeling (e.g. *angry*)
10 another feeling (e.g. *unhappy*)
11 a day of the week (e.g. *Sunday*)
12 a time (e.g. *9 o'clock*)

COMMUNICATION

Look at Activity 11 on p.197. Complete the story with the words that you chose.

See **Extension 28** p.187

29 I've got to stay in ...

A An invitation

1 Listen and practise. (✱ 2.87)

Rick Hey, Donna! How are you doing?
Donna Hey, Rick! Fine.
Rick I'm having a party on Thursday. Would you like to come?
Donna Thursday? I'm sorry, Rick. I can't. I've got to stay in. I've got to revise for an exam.
Rick OK, some other time?
Donna Yes. Great.

2 Look at the tables. Practise with students in your class. Change the words in *italics*.

Invitations

Would you like to	come	*to my party*	*on Saturday?*
	go	*to the cinema*	*tonight?*
	have	*a coffee*	*after the lesson?*

Refusing invitations

Apology	Refusal	Reason	
Sorry,	I can't.	I've got to	*stay in.*
I'm really sorry,	I can't come.	I have to	*revise for an exam.*
I'm afraid	I can't go.		*work.*

> Use **come** for a place where the speaker or listener is now.
> *Will you **come** here, please? OK, I'm **coming** now.*
> We also use **come** for a place where the speaker was, or will be in future.
> *They **came** to my house last week.*
> *Can you **come** to my party tomorrow?*

B Why couldn't you go?

1 **Listen and practise.** (* 2.88)

   Laura Hi, Donna. I didn't see you at Rick's party on Thursday.
   Donna No, I couldn't go.
   Laura Why not?
   Donna I had an exam on Friday. I had to stay in and revise.

UNIVERSITY OF BATLEY
Events November 24th–28th

Monday 24th
Film evening 'The Third Man'

Tuesday 25th: Lecture:
German Philosophy 1820–1900

Wednesday 26th
Pub quiz: Student Union Bar

Thursday 27th: Rock concert:
THE SIRENS + support group

Friday 28th
Karaoke night: Red Lion pub

2 **Listen. Make conversations about the other days.** (* 2.89)

   ▶ I didn't see you at the film on Monday.
   ◀ No, I couldn't go.
   ▶ Why not?
   ◀ I had to go to the gym. I had a fitness test.

C Salim's story

1 Listen and read. (✱ 2.90)

1 I had to leave my country because there was no work. I came to England on my own.

2 I couldn't get a job at first.

3 I couldn't speak English, so I had to go to evening classes.

4 I got a job in a factory. I couldn't spend very much, because I had to save my money.

5 I had to send money home to my parents every month.

6 I worked hard, and I bought a small shop.

7 My shop was open seven days a week, and I had to work every evening.

8 I sold the shop last year. Now I'm retired, and I don't have to work.

2 Pair work. Student A look at the story. Student B look at this page. Ask Student A to correct the information.
1 Salim got a job immediately.
2 He could speak English.
3 He didn't have to go to evening classes.
4 He didn't have to save his money.
5 His parents sent him money.
6 He bought a supermarket.
7 He didn't have to work at weekends.
8 He still has to work.

3 Pair work. Student B look at the story. Student A ask the questions.
1 Why did Salim have to leave his country?
2 Why did he have to go to evening classes?
3 Why couldn't he spend very much money?
4 Why doesn't he work now?

4 Listen. Salim is talking to his grandson, Hashim. ✽ 2.91

What extra information have you learned about Salim?

5 Discuss.
What do older people say about the past in your country?
What things did they have to do?
What things couldn't they do?

---

ability in the present: *can't*
ability in the past: *couldn't*
Could he get a job? Yes, he **could**. /No, he **couldn't**.
He **couldn't** speak English.

obligations in the present: *have / has to* or *'ve / 's got to*
obligations in the past: *had to* NOT ~~had got to~~
Did he **have to** work hard? Yes, he did. /No, he didn't.
He **had to** save.
They didn't **have to** work hard.

D Cultural comparison

1 Read and listen. (✳ 2.92)

Women have to cover their heads in religious buildings. They can't wear short skirts.

You can't drink alcohol until you're twenty-one. Young people have to show ID-cards in restaurants and bars.

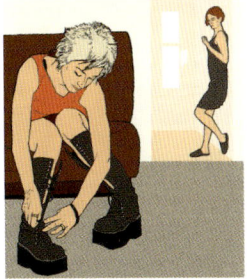

You have to take off your shoes in private homes.

Motorcyclists have to wear crash helmets, but they can't wear them in petrol stations or banks.

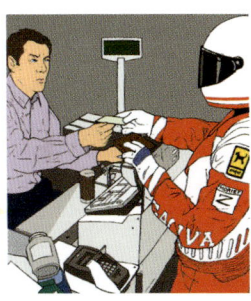

You don't have to show passports when travelling between countries.

You have to give your seat to monks on buses and trains.

2 Ask and answer.
Are these things true in your country?
In which countries are they true?
What other things do people have to do in your country?

COMMUNICATION
Look at Activity 12 on p.198 for more information.

3 Ask and answer.
1 What time do you usually get up?
2 Do you have to get up at that time?
3 What do you usually wear at work?
4 Do have to wear those clothes, or can you wear something different?
5 Do you have to study English? If so, why?

See **Extension 29** p.188

30 What do you want?

A Hopes and fears

1 **Do you think about your future?**
   What are your hopes?
   What are your fears?

2 **Listen. Match the people to the hopes and fears. Do you have similar hopes and fears?** ✴ 2.93

1 I want to be free! I want to leave my job and travel the world.

2 I don't want to go into an old people's home. I really don't.

3 I want to save the world. I want to stop all wars.

4 I want to find a partner. I don't want to be on my own.

5 I want to buy that coat in Harrod's shop window.

6 I want to be the boss. I want to be rich and successful.

B Reasons

1 Pronunciation.
to is /tuː/ before a vowel sound, and /tə/ before a consonant.
u sometimes has a vowel sound /ʌ/: e.g. *understand*.
u sometimes has a consonant sound /juː/: e.g. *use*.

Listen. Which is the sound of *to* in these sentences?
Write A /tuː/, or B /tə/. (✱ 2.94)
1 I want to be a star. ☐
2 I'd like to ask her out. ☐
3 I want to open a bank account. ☐
4 I want to use my English in my job. ☐
5 I'd like to meet some interesting people. ☐
6 I want to enjoy the party tonight. ☐

> *so* and *because*
> I'm not very fit. I want to get fit. I'm going to join a gym.
> ▶ What are you going to do?
> ◀ I want to get fit, **so** I'm going to join a gym.
> Note the comma (,) before *so*.
> ▶ Why are you going to join a gym?
> ◀ I'm going to join a gym **because** I want to get fit.

2 How many sentences can you make with *so*?

I want to be rich	I'm not going to eat chocolate.
I want to get fit	I'm going to take vitamin C.
I'd like to lose weight — **so** —	I'm going to buy a lottery ticket.
I want to be healthy	I'm going to visit the USA.
I want to get a better job	I'm going to join a gym.
I don't want to get a cold	I'm going to revise every night.
I wouldn't like to fail my exams	I'm going to do more exercise.
I want to practise my English	I'm going to work harder.
I'd like to meet some new people	I'm going to take English lessons.

Now join the sentences with *because*.

3 What do you want to do in the next twelve months?
Make a list. Compare your list with a partner.

4 How are you going to do these things?
Make suggestions.

I want to save money, so I'm going to stay in every night.

I'm going to stay in every night because I want to save money.

What I want to do this year
1. Lose weight
2. Get fit
3. Improve my English
4. Save money
5. Have more free time!
6. Get a more interesting job

C Purpose

*He wanted to get some money, **so** he went to the cash machine.*
*He went to the cash machine **because** he wanted to get some money.*
*He went **to get** some money.*

1 **Sam had a lot of things to do yesterday morning. This is his list.**

   buy some flowers
   buy a watch battery
   buy a magazine
   see the doctor
   get a prescription
   get some money
   post some letters
   collect some dry cleaning
   rent a DVD
   buy a phone card

   Look at the pictures and the list, and make conversations. (✳ 2.95)
   ▶ Why did he go to the cash machine?
   ◀ He went to get some money.

2 **Make more conversations. You're at Sam's office.** (✳ 2.96)
   ▶ I'm looking for Sam. Is he here?
   ◀ No, he isn't. He's gone to get some money.

D Learning English: survey

1 Interview another student and complete the questionnaire.

Why are you learning English?
Tick the columns.

- 1 = most important reason
- 2 = very important reason
- 3 = quite important reason
- 4 = not very important
- 5 = not important at all

Reason	1	2	3	4	5
Because I have to.					
Because I want to.					
Because my company / parents want me to.					
So I can get a better job.					
So I can pass an exam.					
So I can travel to English-speaking countries.					
Because I want to live in an English-speaking country.					
Because I enjoy learning languages.					
Because it's something to do in my free time.					
So I can study from books in English.					
So I can use the Internet better.					
So I can speak to tourists / visitors in my country.					

Another reason (write one here):

2 Discuss the results with your class.

3 You've finished this course. Are you going to study more English? Talk about your plans.

See **Extension 30** p.189

**Extensions
Communication activities
Transcripts
Grammar**

EXTENSION 1

Vocabulary

How many English words do you know?
Add more countries and nationalities to the table.

Country	Nationality		
Mexico	Mexican	-an	
Italy	Italian	-ian	
Turkey	Turkish	-ish	
Japan	Japanese	-ese	
Pakistan	Pakistani	-i	
France	French	other	

Personal information

Men
married = Mr
single = Mr

Women
married = Mrs
single = Miss
don't know = Ms

Put this information in Column A.

Smith   0282 594 3016   Diana   British   *Diana Smith*   Ms

	A	B
Title (Mr, Ms, Mrs, Miss)		
Family name		
First name		
Nationality		
Telephone number		
Signature		

Now add your information to Column B.

Culture: names

You say ...	You don't say ...	
Hello, Peter.	~~Hello, Mr Peter.~~	~~Hello, Smith.~~
Hello, Mr Smith.	~~Hello, Peter Smith.~~	~~Hello, Mr Peter Smith.~~

In your language, which do you say ...?

/e/	yes spell ten hello next American seven lesson
/aɪ/	my Hi five I Ireland nice Kylie Bye Goodbye

EXTENSION 2

Text messages

CUL8R is a text message.
It means 'See you later'.
C is for *see*, U is for *you*,
L8 is for *late*, L8R is for *later*.

Match the text abbreviations and their meanings.

Abbreviation	Meaning	Abbreviation	Meaning
ru?	please	luv	to, too
ur	be	2nite	love
pls	message	2	great
thx	are you?	4u	Bye for now.
xxx	you are	bfn	for you
b	kisses	gr8	I'm
idk	thanks	im	tonight
msg	I don't know.		

Read these messages. What do they mean?

> msg. ruok.4.2nite?
> bfn.luvu. dave. xxx

> gr8.cu2nite, thx.
> luvu2. anna.

Review

Tick the correct answers.
1. Are you British? ☐ Yes, they are. ☐ No, I'm a student. ☐ No, I'm not.
2. Where are you from? ☐ We're from Italy. ☐ I'm a tourist. ☐ I'm here.
3. How old is she? ☐ She's fine. ☐ She's about twenty-five. ☐ She's old.
4. What's your phone number? ☐ Yes, it's my phone number. ☐ 366 9008. ☐ You're over eighteen.
5. How are you? ☐ Fine, thanks. ☐ I'm Spanish. ☐ Goodbye.
6. What's your nationality? ☐ Australia. ☐ Brazilian. ☐ Yes, I am.

Conversation

Number these sentences in the correct order and make a conversation.
☐ And how are your children?
☐ I'm very well, thanks, Sarah. And you?
☐ Good afternoon, David. How are you?
☐ They're fine, thank you.
☐ I'm fine.

/æ/	am	and	that	married	family	nationality	Spanish	accent
/eɪ/	name	great	eight	late	table	they	stay	Australia	USA

EXTENSION 3

Vocabulary

Add words to these phrases.
a slice of ... ham
a pot of ...
a cup of ...
a glass of ...
a bottle of ...
a can of ...
a slice of ...

What's your favourite?

Ask and answer.
What's your favourite hot drink?
What's your favourite cold drink?
What's your favourite fast food?
What's your favourite sandwich?

Connecting

Match the questions and the answers.
Ask the questions. Say the answers.

Question	Answer
1 Anything else?	A Fine, thanks.
2 How are you?	B Two twenty.
3 Are you hungry?	C No, thanks. That's all.
4 How old are you?	D France.
5 How much is it?	E No, French.
6 Where are you from?	F I'm twenty-two.
7 Is the wine Spanish?	G No, I'm not.

| /iː/ | me | he | we | she | please | tea | eat | see | cheese | meet | pizza |
| /ɪ/ | it | is | drink | six | listen | single | still | sandwich | English | Miss | |

EXTENSION 4

Spotlight: *a, an, the*
Remember, the sound of the next word is important, not the spelling.

an **um**brella /ʌm/   a **un**iversity /juː/   an **or**ange /ɒr/   a **eu**ro /jʊə/
a **wi**ndow /wɪ/   a **o**ne-dollar bill /wʌ/   a **D**VD /diː/   an **M**P3 /em/

1 Choose *a* or *an*.

.... car	.... American car	.... black umbrella
.... umbrella	.... European car	.... old black umbrella
.... idea	.... good idea	.... university student
.... UFO	.... A320 plane	.... IBM computer

2 Choose *a*, *an*, or *the*.
1 My cup's on .... table.
2 I'm .... student.
3 Mr Smith is .... teacher of Class 5.
4 The Warhol paintings are in .... Museum of Modern Art.
5 The Mondrian painting is in .... art museum in Germany.

Strategies: using your dictionary
The plural of most words is + -s.   *star – star**s**   apple – apple**s***
The dictionary helps you when there are different plural spellings.

city /ˈsɪti/ *noun* (*plural* **cities**)
1 a big and important town: *the city of Liverpool* ◇ *the city centre*

tomato /təˈmɑːtəʊ/ *noun* (*plural* **tomatoes**)
a soft red fruit that you cook or eat in salads: *tomato soup*

watch¹ /wɒtʃ/ *noun* (*plural* **watches**)
a thing that shows what time it is. You wear a watch on your wrist.

key¹ /kiː/ *noun*
1 a piece of metal that opens or closes a lock: *He turned the key and opened the door.*

Find the plurals of these words.

address   baby   box   bus   country   kilo   piano   potato   story

Spelling rule: Add -*es* to words ending in -*s*, -*ss*, -*ch*, -*x*.
Some words ending in -*o* are + -*s*, some are + -*es*.

Large numbers

100	a hundred / one hundred	1000	a thousand / one thousand
200	two hundred	3000	three thousand
157	one hundred and fifty-seven	5,700	five thousand, seven hundred
4,398	four thousand, three hundred and ninety-eight		

Write these numbers in words. Say them aloud.
400   650   864   913   10,000   1400   1673   5422

/s/	artist**s** coat**s** cup**s** hat**s** plate**s** seat**s** ship**s** ticket**s**
/z/	apple**s** bed**s** bird**s** chair**s** row**s** star**s** table**s** train**s** tree**s**
/ɪz/	watch**es** bus**es** box**es** class**es** sandwich**es** orang**es** entranc**es**

EXTENSION 5

Culture: gadgets

British 'Tweens' (kids between 8 and 12), and their parents, spend three billion pounds a year on gadgets.

	Girls %	Boys %
video games console	37	81
television	55	77
radio	70	60
CD player	68	60
video recorder	33	39
mobile phone	23	24
PC (Personal Computer)	10	16
Internet connection (anywhere in the home)	33	35

What have they got? Make sentences about the table.
60% (sixty per cent) of boys have got a CD player.

Are there any children in your family? What gadgets have they got?

Spotlight: *got*

**In informal English, some people say *have / has got* as *got*.
In some songs, they write *got*.
Rewrite these song titles with *have / has got*.**

- I Got You Babe *Sonny and Cher*
- You Got It *Roy Orbison*
- I Got Rhythm *Ella Fitzgerald*
- She Got The Look *Statetrooper*

Strategies: using your dictionary

child /tʃaɪld/ *noun* (*plural* **children** /'tʃɪldrən/)
1 a boy or girl: *There are 30 children in the class.*
2 a daughter or son: *One of her children got married last year.*

Find the plurals of these words.

| child | grandchild | man | woman | wife | *children* |

| /ɒ/ | got | hot | pot | sorry | bottle | o'clock | orange | on | chocolate |
| /əʊ/ | no | don't | phone | closed | know | window | yellow | espresso |

EXTENSION 6

Reading: adverts

Read the adverts and find:
a part-time job
a holiday job
a dangerous job
a temporary job

Knife-thrower's Assistant urgently required. Ability to stand very still is important. Tel: Walton's Circus, 07861 110055

Server for fast-food restaurant. Three evenings a week, 7–11. No weekends. City centre. Tel: World Burger, 020 4536 7891

Lifeguard required for summer holidays. June 7th – September 15th Tel: Beach Office, 01202 109361

Temporary secretaries for 1 to 14 days. Excellent pay. Tel: INSTANT OFFICE AGENCY 023 1999 5577

Culture: part-time jobs

Complete the sentences.
My friend Ryan is .... student. He's .... a part-time job. He works .... a fast-food restaurant in the evenings. He works three evenings .... week. He doesn't work .... weekends. He sells burgers .... hot-dogs.

Do students in your country have part-time jobs?
Talk about your friends and people in your family. What do they do?

Word + word

Add these words to the word map. Can you add more?

weekends   London   a big company   an office   8 to 6   home
Monday to Friday   Sony   a factory

| /uː/ | do | to | you | blue | too | room | two | who | school |
| /ʌ/ | does | unemployed | company | cousin | country | bus | Monday |

EXTENSION 7

Reading: Too many clocks ...

HOW MANY CLOCKS have you got? And how many do you need? There are four clocks in my kitchen. There's one on the wall, another on the cooker, and a third on the microwave. I've got a small radio in the kitchen, and there's a clock on that too. I wear a watch, and my husband and both my children wear watches. So when we're all in the kitchen, there are eight clocks in one room. And then there's the living room. We've got a clock on the wall, and there's a clock on the video recorder. The telephone's got a clock, the computer's got a clock and the radio's got a clock too. We've all got alarm clocks in our bedrooms. There's only one problem. They all show different times!

How many clocks are there in your home? Make a list.

Review

Tick (✔) the sentences that are true for you. Correct the ones that aren't true.
1. There are fifteen students in my class.
2. There's a football stadium in my town.
3. There isn't a cafeteria in my school.
4. There isn't a McDonald's in my town.
5. There aren't any mountains in my country.
6. There are some factories near the school.

Word + word

Which words do you think of first? Underline one example. (All the words are correct.)

city	city centre city police New York City inner city
shopping	shopping centre shopping mall shopping bag shopping hours
football	football club football team football stadium football results
international	international word international airport international news international hotel
telephone	telephone book telephone number mobile telephone telephone operator

/aʊ/	town down now how south mountain county thousand
/ɔː/	or port north airport for four boring all mall call football wall

EXTENSION 8

Reading: signs

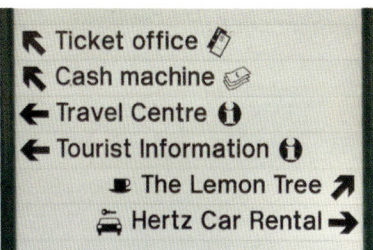

Find answers to these questions on the signs.
1. How many platforms are there at Bath Spa station?
2. Do trains to London leave from platform one?
3. Where do trains to the North of England leave from?
4. Can you get money at the station? Where?
5. What is 'The Lemon Tree'?

Spotlight: time

**Complete the clock.
Write in the times.**

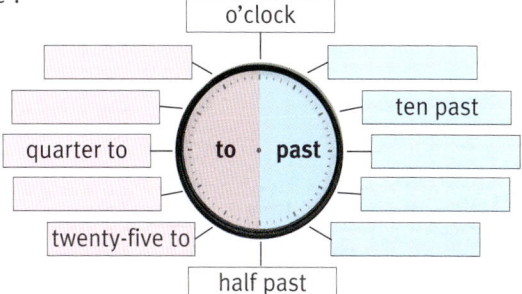

Culture: times

Complete with these words.

half past five   in the afternoon   seven   seventeen hundred

- In Britain, people use the 12-hour clock in conversation, but the 24-hour clock for timetables. In the 24-hour clock, 5 o'clock in the afternoon is ....

- In the USA, the military use the 24-hour clock, but timetables use the 12-hour clock. Five o'clock in the morning is *5 a.m.* and 5 o'clock .... is *5 p.m.* On timetables, they sometimes write just *5.00 a.* and *5.00 p.*

- In both the UK and USA, *five thirty* is becoming more common than .... because there are more digital clocks.

- A new expression is *24/7* (*twenty-four seven*). It means 'all the time' (twenty-four hours a day, ... days a week). E.g. *You can text me twenty-four seven.*

| /ɑː/ | are | car | father | cards | depart | past | passport | half | answer |
| /ɜː/ | her | person | early | work | word | sir | bird | thirty | thirteen |

Reading: instructions

Number the instructions in the correct order from 1 to 6.

☐ Please select the amount you require.
  ☐ 10 ☐ 20 ☐ 50 ☐ 100 ☐ 200
  ☐ OTHER Enter the amount.

☐ Please take your cash. Thank you for using Southern Bank.

☐ Please enter your PIN number now.

☐ Please select a service.
  ☐ Cash only   ☐ Cash with receipt
  ☐ Balance of your account   ☐ Request new cheque book

☐ Welcome to Southern Bank Cash Machine.
  Please insert your card now.

☐ Please remove your card now, and wait for your cash.

Number puzzle

Instructions:

A Put a four in the bottom right corner.
B Put a nine in the middle square of the right column.
C Put a six at the top of the left column.
D Put a three in the middle of the bottom row.
E Put a two in the top right corner.
F Put a seven between the six and the two.
G Put a five in the middle square.
H Put a one next to the five.
I Put an eight in the last square.

left column	middle column	right column	diagonal
			top row
			middle row
		4	bottom row

Look at this.

1 + 3 = 4 (one plus three equals four)
Add up the rows.   Add up the columns.   Add up the diagonals.
What are the answers?

| /ʊ/ | put | look | book | cook | good | football | woman | cookbook |
| /ʌ/ | up | cup | but | butter | much | Russia | lovely | some | colour |

EXTENSION 10

Culture: ages

13	get a part-time job
16	leave school
	get a full-time job
	join the army, navy or air-force
	get married with your parents' permission
	ride a motorbike (under 50 c.c.)
	buy cigarettes
17	drive a car
18	get married without permission
	buy alcohol
	vote in elections
	buy a house
	see any film
21	drive a truck (HGV or *heavy goods vehicle*)
	be an MP (Member of Parliament)

Look at the list of ages for Britain. Ask and answer.
▶ At what age can you buy alcohol in Britain?
◀ In Britain, you can buy alcohol at eighteen.
In the USA, you can't buy alcohol until you are twenty-one.

Make sentences about your country.
In my country you can buy cigarettes at …

Permission

What can you do in class? Make sentences.
We can / can't use a mobile phone in class.

use a mobile phone	use a dictionary	play cards	smoke
speak (your language)	wear jeans	eat	
listen to a Walkman	chew gum	translate	

Review

Can you do these things in English?

Can you count down from 20 to 11? Can you name five nationalities?
Can you say the days of the week? Can you name five colours?
Can you say the alphabet? Can you tell the time?

| /æ/ | stressed sound for *a* | can | have | has | am | camera | Canada |
| /ə/ | unstressed sound for *a* | can | have | has | am | camera | Canada |

Strategies: when you don't know the word

that / those

this / these

Are the things on the buffet countable or uncountable? Guess. Write *C* or *U* next to the pictures.

Do you know the words for these things? If not, you can just point and say:

> Some of this, please.

> Some of that, please.

Uncountable: *some of this / some of that*
Countable: *some of these / some of those / one of these / two of those*

Imagine you're at the buffet. Point and ask.

Vocabulary: diets

What can people eat on these diets? What can't people eat on these diets? Choose one diet and make a list.

A low-cholesterol / low-fat diet   A vegetarian diet
A non-dairy diet   A high-protein diet

Spotlight: *Who? / Who's? / Whose?*

Complete the sentences with *Who, Who's* or *Whose*.

1 '.................. got a car?' 'Maria has.'
2 '.................. shoes are these?' 'They're Mark's shoes.'
3 '.................. lives in that flat?' 'Philip does.'
4 '.................. mother works in a bank?' 'Chloe's mother.'
5 '.................. a vegetarian?' 'Jason is.'
6 '.................. works for Microsoft?' 'Karen does.'

/ɪə/	near	dear	hear	beer	here	we're	idea	
/eə/	air	where	there	they're	their	chair	pair	careful	wear

Conversation

Complete the words on the last picture.

Culture: *I'd like* v. *I want*

Requests and offers

I'd like that one, please. is more polite than *I want that one, please.*
Would you like a pen? is more polite than *Do you want a pen?*
Remember that in requests the tone of your voice is more important than the words you choose.
You can say *Do you want a pen?* in a friendly, polite voice.
You can say *I'd like a pen.* in an unfriendly, impolite voice.

Review: *How much ...? / How many ...?*

How many questions can you make?

How	much ...	students	have they got?
	many ...	kilometres	can you play?
		sugar	is there in the can?
		money	can you speak?
		musical instruments	have you got?
		languages	a week do you travel?
		beer	are there in your class?
		chocolates	would you like?
		children	do you want?

/ʃ/	she	ship	shop	shower	push	fish	dish	wash	mashed
/tʃ/	chair	chips	cheese	choices	children	much	beach	watch	

EXTENSION 13

Souvenirs

Match the words and pictures. You're buying presents for your family and friends. Make conversations. Change the words in *italics*.

> a model bus   a model London taxi   a T-shirt   a football scarf
> a tin of English tea   some socks   a coffee mug   a baseball cap
> a Beefeater doll

Assistant Can I help you?
Tourist I'm looking for a present.
Assistant Who's it for?
Tourist It's for *my grandmother*.
Assistant Hmm. How about *a tin of English tea*?

Stressed form: Who's it for /fɒr/?
Unstressed form: I'm looking for /fə/ a present.

What are typical souvenirs from your country?

Spotlight: *about*

Put *about* into these sentences.
I think it's two kilometres. *I think it's about two kilometres.*

1 I think she's fifteen.
2 It takes ten minutes.
3 It's twelve o'clock.
4 Have you got any information bus times?
5 She can't see you on Friday. How Saturday?
6 It's fifty euros.

Word + word

Make word maps for *in* and *on* with these words.

> the east   the beach   the left
> the country   the radio   the third row
> the second floor   the middle   a factory
> London   the floor   the living room

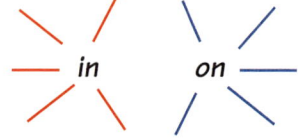

| /n/ | in | on | man | men | woman | women | children | tin | then | one |
| /ŋ/ | looking | trying | walking | talking | going | sing | along | thing | | |

EXTENSION 14

Imagine: What are you doing?

Pair work. Student A: Choose one of these places and imagine you are there. Tell your partner. Student B: Ask questions and guess what Student A is doing.

a department store   the beach   a cinema   a restaurant   a night club
the bathroom   a sports stadium   a train   an airport   a gymnasium

► I'm in the cinema.
◄ Are you watching a film?
► Yes, I am.
◄ What are you watching?
► I'm watching 'Star Wars III'.
◄ Are you eating something?
► No, I'm not.
◄ Who are you sitting next to?
► I'm sitting next to my boyfriend.
◄ Are you holding hands?
► No, we aren't …

Connecting

Each sentence in column B continues from a sentence in column A. Match them.

A
1 This is a South-West Trains announcement.
2 Please be quiet.
3 She can't speak now.
4 Don't change the channel!
5 It's the 87th minute.
6 No, thank you.
7 Can you help me?

B
A She's having a shower.
B I'm enjoying this programme.
C And United are winning by two goals to nil.
D I'm just looking.
E The 10.42 from London Waterloo is now arriving at platform three.
F My e-mail program isn't working.
G The children are sleeping.

Spelling

Put the -ing forms of these verbs in the table.

give work phone hide talk listen sit stand serve look try
put hold feed take wear eat drink enjoy tell shop wave

+ -ing	do – doing
– e, + -ing	have – having
double the last letter + -ing	stop – stopping

/ɔɪ/ noise boy enjoy toy oil point unemployed Rolls-Royce

/ɔː/ or fourth law daughter walk floor store your door

EXTENSION 15

Strategies: grammar books

Present simple for likes and dislikes

- The verbs *like*, *love*, and *hate* are not used in the present continuous form.
  I like tea. NOT *I'm liking tea.*
- Don't use *I like …* / *Do you like …?* for requests or offers.
  Use *I'd like …* for requests. Use *Would you like …?* for offers.
- Use *like*, *love*, and *hate* for positive sentences about likes and dislikes.
  Use *don't like* for negative sentences.
  You can use *love* and *hate* in the negative, but only in personal situations!
  I don't love you any more.   I don't hate you, but I don't love you either.
  NOT *I don't love coffee.*
- *like*, *love*, and *hate* are often followed by an *-ing* form.
  I like running.   I hate swimming.

Read the text from a grammar book. Is it easy or difficult?
Do you understand more after reading it? Now do this exercise.
Look at the text to help you. Choose the correct words.
1 They (don't / doesn't) like the hotel.
2 He (likes / is liking) learning English.
3 They don't like (swimming / swim) on cold days.
4 I don't (like / love) hamburgers.
5 (Do / Would) you like a biscuit?

Word + word

Put the words in the table.

| exercise   tennis   aerobics   chess   yoga   basketball   martial arts |

I like playing …	
I like doing …	

Review: requests and offers

Read the sentences. Tick (✔) the requests. Underline the offers.
The other sentences are questions.
1 Can I have some bread, please?
2 Have you got any English cheese?
3 Would you like some ice in your drink?
4 I'd like an espresso, please.
5 Do you like strong coffee?
6 Is there any milk in the fridge?

| /θ/ | thanks | three | thirty | theatre | Thursday | think | nothing |
| /ð/ | this | that | these | those | they | the | there | then | brother |

EXTENSION 16

Culture: informal English

Read the dictionary definition. Rewrite these song titles with the full forms.

gonna
/ˈgənə/ (informal) a way of writing 'going to' to show that sb is speaking in an informal way or with a special accent ☛ Do not write 'gonna' yourself because it might be marked as a mistake. **wanna** (= want to) and **gotta** (= 've got to) are similar.

- Everything's gonna be alright *Sweetbox*
- I wanna be your man *The Beatles*
- You gotta move *The Rolling Stones*
- I'm gonna be strong *Gene Pitney*
- Do you wanna dance? *Cliff Richard*
- Gotta travel on *Trini Lopez*
- If you wanna be happy *Jimmy Soul*

Connecting

Make sentences with *from*.

1. This birthday card's
2. The office is open
3. The Cardiff train is leaving
4. He comes
5. We're going to be on holiday
6. We can see London Bridge
7. I'm flying
8. Can you translate *restaurant*

from

- A July 7th to July 21st.
- B 9 to 5.
- C our hotel window.
- D my uncle.
- E Heathrow to New York.
- F platform two.
- G English to French?
- H Japan.

Spotlight: zero

Topic	Write	Say
temperature	0°C	**zero** degrees Celsius
football	Arsenal 2, Liverpool 0	Arsenal two, Liverpool **nil**.
tennis	30 – 0	thirty – **love**
phone number	020 7300	**o** two **o**, seven three double **o**
numbers	0	**zero** or **nought**
years	2004	two thousand and four
	2109	twenty one **o** nine

| /i/ | wind**y** | cloud**y** | sunn**y** | happ**y** | bus**y** | earl**y** | fift**y** | eight**y** | ninet**y** |
| /aɪ/ | b**y** | m**y** | wh**y** | fl**y** | tr**y** | goodb**y**e | t**y**pe | b**uy** | g**uy** |

EXTENSION 17

Past times

Choose a time in your past. Talk about it.

1956 I was eight years old. I was at school in Bristol in England. There were thirty children in my class. My teacher's name was Miss Dodds. She was very nice. My best friend was Janet Roberts. We were friends for two or three years.

Dates

Answer the questions.
Which dates do you remember every year?
Are they birthdays? National holidays? Anniversaries? Tax payment dates? The start or end of a college course? Make a list.

Word + word

Which words can go with *last* and *next*?
Delete the words that can't follow *last* or *next*.

this	week	month	8.30	morning	year	now		
last	night	yesterday	day	week	month	September	year	2004
next	tomorrow	9.15	week	day	month	February	year	2006

Review: the sound /ə/

The unstressed sound /ə/ is the most common vowel sound in English.

Look at these sentences, and choose the correct sound.
1. A They weren't at her party. /wɜː/ or /wə/
   B Yes, they were! /wɜː/ or /wə/
2. A She was eighteen last birthday. /wɒz/ or /wəz/
   B No, she wasn't! /wɒz/ or /wəz/
3. A Can you speak French? /kæn/ or /kən/
   B Yes, I can. /kæn/ or /kən/
4. A Are you going to see her next week? /tuː/ or /tə/
   B I've got two tickets for the concert. /tuː/ or /tə/
5. A Have you got the time? /hæv/ or /həv/
   B No, I haven't got a watch. /hæv/ or /həv/
6. A Is that for me? Thank you. /fɔː/ or /fə/
   B What are you looking for? /fɔː/ or /fə/

/ɒ/	was	got	watch	modern	boss	clock	October	job	model
/ɜː/	were	her	first	third	thirtieth	shirt	early	work	word

EXTENSION 18

Reading: facts in a text

Read the text.
Amber Keane is a rock singer. She tells this story about her first record.

> 'Midnight Groove' wasn't a big hit in Britain, but it got into the Top 40 in New Zealand. It got to number 32, I think. Anyway, I went to New Zealand for a concert tour. I didn't have much money in those days, and I flew in Economy Class. I was on the plane for 25 hours. I saw about seven films, and I had five meals. The plane landed in Auckland. I got off the plane, and there were about two thousand people at the airport. There were photographers and reporters everywhere. It was fantastic! I felt wonderful! Then I saw him. Prince William came out of the door from First Class. The crowd and the photographers were for him, not me. I felt really stupid. There was nobody to meet me. I went to the terminal and got a bus to my hotel.

Write sentences about the text with these numbers.

40   32   25   7   5   2000

40 'Midnight Groove' got into the Top 40 in New Zealand.

Spotlight: *get / got*

Complete the sentences with *get* or *got*.
1 Take your umbrella. Don't .... wet.
2 He .... food poisoning, but she didn't.
3 She's going to .... married next year.
4 I .... three birthday cards yesterday.
5 Have you .... the time?
6 We went to the supermarket and .... some food.
7 Does Amber .... many letters from her fans?
8 The Beatles' first record didn't .... into the Top 10 in England.

Connecting

Make sentences with *for*.

1 We went   A the birthday present.
2 He was asleep   B a walk on the beach.
3 Is that coffee   C breakfast.
4 Thank you   *for*   D twelve hours.
5 They went to Canada   E me? Thank you.
6 I had a boiled egg   F their honeymoon.

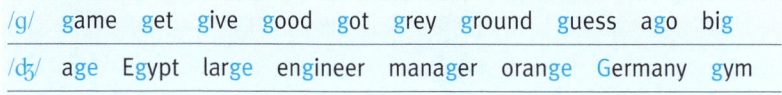

| /g/ | game | get | give | good | got | grey | ground | guess | ago | big |
| /dʒ/ | age | Egypt | large | engineer | manager | orange | Germany | gym |

EXTENSION 19

Reading: irregular verbs

The Grammar Doctor answers your questions …

Q Why are some verbs irregular?
A The common everyday verbs are often irregular – **went**, **came**, etc. But don't worry. Most verbs are regular. All new verbs are regular, e.g. **e-mailed**, **faxed**, **scanned**. English children learn to say **went** and **came** when they are very young. Then, when they're five or six, they understand the regular-verb rule. They try to make all verbs regular and make mistakes. They say **goed** and **comed**.

Q Do I need to learn lots of irregular verbs?
A There are about 200 in English. Fifty per cent of them are not very important. You can ask questions, give short answers, and give negative answers without knowing the irregular verb. But try to learn new ones when you meet them.

Q What happens with new verbs when I don't know the past?
A Guess that they are regular. If you're wrong, people will understand it's the past. Check in a dictionary. Irregular verbs are noted.

Find the past tenses of these verbs in a dictionary.

| say | know | give | understand | make |

Vocabulary

Complete the sentences with these words.

| died | married | divorced | born | engaged |

1 Charles and Diana got .... in February 1981.
2 They got .... on 29 July 1981.
3 Prince William was .... on 21 June 1982.
4 They got .... in 1996.
5 She .... in Paris on 31 August 1997.

Spelling: regular verbs

| **add -ed** want – wanted | **add -d** move – moved |
| **change -y to -ied** study – studied | **double letters** stop – stopped |

Write the past of these regular verbs.

| like | try | need | walk | scan | cry | hate | want | wash | reply |

/d/	phoned	moved	travelled	listened	died	opened	closed
/t/	danced	worked	asked	liked	walked	passed	looked
/ɪd/	needed	decided	wanted	selected	adopted	hated

EXTENSION 20

Strategies: organizing past verbs

How can you organize past verbs in your vocabulary notebook?
Look at these ways. You can use all of them. Which ones do you prefer?

- **Opposites**
  came – went, gave – took, lifted – dropped, arrived – left
- **Irregular verbs with the same sound and spelling in the past**
  bought, brought, thought   drew, flew, knew
- **Irregular verbs with a change in the vowel sound only**
  come – came, draw – drew, drink – drank, fall – fell, get – got,
  give – gave, hold – held, know – knew, meet – met, run – ran,
  sing – sang, write – wrote
- **Irregular verbs with no change in the past**
  cut – cut, put – put
- **Regular verbs with the same spelling rule**
  Double the letter: drop – dropped, rob – robbed, stop – stopped
  '-y' to '-ied': carry – carried, study – studied

Some verbs aren't in easy groups! Write the past of these verbs.

go   do   have   feel   leave   say   send

Spotlight: nouns and adjectives

It's worth five pounds. (*pounds* is a plural noun)
It's a five-pound note. (*pound* is an adjective. Adjectives are singular).

Choose the correct word.
1 Chris is a seventeen- (year / years) -old boy.
2 The teenage robbers were sixteen (year / years) old.
3 It was a 200- (mile / miles) journey to Harrogate.
4 Chris went ten (metre / metres) into the air.
5 It was a sixty- (minute / minutes) videotape.
6 We waited for twenty (minute / minutes).

Review

a 700-megabyte CDR / an 80-minute CDR
a one-euro coin / a two-euro coin

Complete with *a* or *an*. Think about the sound of the next word.
1 .... 650-megabyte CDR
2 .... 18-year-old girl
3 .... 94-year-old man
4 .... 11-kilometre walk
5 .... one-mile journey
6 .... 800-mile flight

| /uː/ | flew | drew | lose | into | onto | you | too | two | food |
| /ɔː/ | bought | brought | thought | draw | saw | water | Shaun | born |

EXTENSION 21

Student evaluation

Are you a good student?
Complete this form about your partner.

Student's name		always	usually	sometimes	hardly ever	never
1	How often is he/she on time for class?	5	4	3	2	1
2	How often does he/she do his/her homework?	5	4	3	2	1
3	Is his/her homework correct?	5	4	3	2	1
4	Is he/she happy in the lesson?	5	4	3	2	1
5	Does he/she answer questions in class?	5	4	3	2	1
6	Does he/she remember all his/her books, pens, paper etc.?	5	4	3	2	1
	Total score					

Word order

Frequency adverbs come before the main verb.
I usually get up at 7.30. I don't often listen to the radio.
But they come after the verb *to be*.
It's usually hot in July. She's hardly ever late for class.

Put the words in the correct order.
1 class. / He / for / is / late / sometimes
2 day. / eats / always / She / apple / an / a
3 often / in / They / restaurants. / eat / don't
4 January / England. / in / in / usually / It / cold / is
5 late. / trains / sometimes / British / are

Spotlight: *How?*

How many questions can you make? (– = no word)

How	old	are you?
	often	is it?
	many	days a week do you work?
	much	do you watch TV in the evenings?
	about	Monday 27th at 10.30?
	long	do you pronounce this word?
	(–)	does the journey take?

/j/	yes yesterday yellow your young
/juː/	unit euro Europe university excuse me you
/dʒ/	jeans jacket jewellery juice Japanese join January orange

EXTENSION 22

Culture: British and American English

Some everyday words for clothes are different in British and American English. But don't worry, people in both Britain and the USA usually understand all of them. For example, you see both *pants* and *trousers* in the USA. What's the difference? None, really. But if you can put them in a washing machine, they're usually *pants*. If you take them to a dry-cleaner they're usually *trousers*.

Find the words in your dictionary. Does it mark the words US and GB/UK?

pants	undershorts
trousers	pants
waistcoat	vest
vest	undershirt
handbag	purse
trainers	sneakers
jewellery	jewelry
tights	pantyhose

Review

Read the answers. Tick (✔) the correct question.

Answers   **Questions**

1 Blonde.
    A What colour are her eyes? ☐
    B What colour is her hair? ☐
    C What colour is her top? ☐

2 Yes, she has.
    A Has she got long hair? ☐
    B Does she wear glasses? ☐
    C Is she wearing a hat? ☐

3 He's very handsome.
    A What's he wearing? ☐
    B Has he got a moustache? ☐
    C What does he look like? ☐

4 Yes, he does.
    A What does he like? ☐
    B Does he like wearing suits? ☐
    C What does he look like? ☐

5 Yes, she is.
    A Does she usually wear a uniform? ☐
    B Is she wearing a uniform? ☐
    C Has she got a uniform? ☐

6 Medium.
    A What size are you? ☐
    B How are you? ☐
    C How old are you? ☐

/ɑː/	glasses dance scarf hardly martial arts laughed demand
/æ/	had attractive handsome African casual habit alcohol

EXTENSION 23

Review

Has anybody in your class done these things? Find out. Ask five people. Put a tick (✓) for yes, put a cross (✗) for no.

been to California?	☐	☐	☐	☐	☐
seen a Harry Potter film?	☐	☐	☐	☐	☐
seen a tarantula?	☐	☐	☐	☐	☐
been on a jumbo jet?	☐	☐	☐	☐	☐
seen a film in English?	☐	☐	☐	☐	☐

Foreign visitors

Imagine you are talking to a visitor to your country. Here are some useful questions. Match the questions and the answers.

Question
1. Have you been here before?
2. Is this your first visit?
3. How long have you been here?
4. What do you think of (my country)?
5. How many times have you been here?
6. Have you seen the (famous building) yet?
7. Have you been to (an interesting place) yet?

Answer
A No, I've been here before.
B No, I haven't seen it yet.
C Yes, I have. I was here five years ago.
D Three times.
E Not yet. I want to go there next week.
F It's very interesting.
G About two weeks.

Role play a conversation with a foreign visitor.

Word + word

Which words do you think of first? Underline one example. (All the words are correct.)

rock	rock singer	rock 'n' roll	rock concert	rocking chair
phone	mobile phone (UK)	cellphone (USA)	phone box	phone card
park	theme park	national park	car park	park and ride
hair	blonde hair	long hair	curly hair	short hair

| /iː/ | been | seen | meet | scene | teenage | clean | beach | teacher | sea |
| /eɪ/ | date | hate | place | day | say | pay | way | May | painting | famous |

EXTENSION 24

Review

Choose the correct words to complete the sentences.
I (am coming / come) from Poland, but I (am studying / study) in England at the moment. I (arrived / have arrived) two months ago and I'm (going / to go) home next month. I've (been / went) to a lot of different places in England. I ('ve been / am going) to Oxford twice, and I (was / 've been) to Stratford once. I've (saw / seen) Shakespeare's house. I (haven't been / didn't go) to London yet. I'm (going / have been) there next Saturday. I (am liking / like) England, but I miss my family.

Spotlight: frequency adverbs

Make these sentences true for you.
Put *often*, *sometimes*, or *never* in the spaces.
1. I've .... travelled to foreign countries.
2. I've .... cooked a meal for ten people.
3. I've .... been to the Moon.
4. I've .... stayed in a hotel.
5. I've .... swum in the sea.
6. I've .... come first in a race.
7. I've .... been late for class.
8. I've .... run 1000 metres.
9. I've .... slept in a tent.

Past participles

Look at the past participles in *Spotlight*. Make a table in your notebook, like this.

Infinitive	travel					
Past simple	travelled					
Past participle	travelled	cooked	come	run	swum	slept

| /n/ past participles | been | seen | gone | done | flown | eaten |
| /ŋ/ present participles | being | seeing | going | doing | flying | eating |

EXTENSION 25

Apologizing

When we say 'sorry' we usually add something. Look.

Apology	What can you add?	Examples
Sorry, I'm sorry, I'm very sorry, I'm really sorry,	an excuse	I forgot. it was an accident. I didn't see you.
	a promise	it won't happen again. I'll be careful next time.
	an offer	I'll buy you another one. I'll do it now.

Apologize in these situations.
1 You're late for work.
2 You haven't done your homework.
3 You've lost a friend's pen.
4 You've taken someone's seat in a café.
5 You've walked through a door in front of an old lady.

Useful expressions

**Someone invites you to a party.
You can't decide. What can you say?**

I'm not sure. I don't know.	I'll see.
	I'll think about it.
	I'll tell you later. I'll let you know. I'll call you tomorrow.

Reply to these questions.
1 Are you coming to my party on Saturday?
2 Would you like to come for a drink this evening?
3 Why don't you go to the doctor?
4 Can you help me tomorrow evening?

Spotlight: contractions

Write contractions of these words.

will	have	has	did not	are	do not	would
will not	have not	has not	does not	are not	cannot	would not

| /l/ | I'll | He'll | She'll | will | small | really | later | landlord | lights | play |
| /r/ | sorry | worry | marry | terrible | boring | scenery | right | receive | | |

EXTENSION 26

Making predictions

Make predictions.

a Weather forecaster   b Newscaster   c Football reporter

Think about tomorrow's weather. What will it be like?
I think it'll be warm. I don't think it'll rain.

Think about stories in the news this week. What will happen next?
I think there'll be problems at the airports.
I don't think the Prince will marry her.

Think about sports matches next weekend. Who will win?
I don't think England will beat Scotland.
I think Newcastle will lose to Manchester United.

Making decisions

Make sentences about these times with *I think ...* / *I don't think ...*

| now   at 11 o'clock   after the lesson   later today   on Saturday |
| tomorrow morning   next year   tonight |

I think I'll have a cup of coffee now.
I don't think I'll go out tonight.

Review

Complete the sentences with true facts about you.
1 I'll be .... next birthday.
2 My (brother) will be .... next birthday.
3 I'll be seventy years old in 20 ....
4 I'll finish this English book ....
5 We won't be at school next ....
6 I'll see .... this evening.

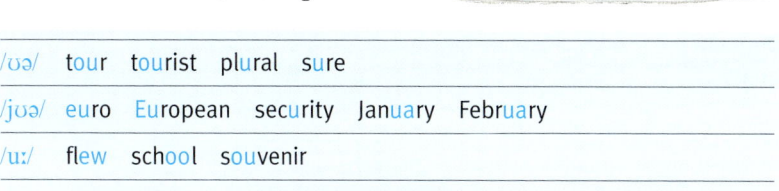

/ʊə/	tour tourist plural sure
/jʊə/	euro European security January February
/uː/	flew school souvenir
/juː/	future few usually music queue

EXTENSION 27

The best places in town

A visitor is asking you about your town. Answer the questions.

What's the oldest building?
What's the most modern building?
What's the most beautiful building?
What's the most interesting place?
Where are the best shops?
Where are the most expensive clothes shops?
What's the largest supermarket?
What's the best restaurant?

Compare your answers with your partner.

▶ The cathedral's the oldest building.
◀ I don't agree. I think the castle's older than the cathedral.

Guggenheim Art Museum, Bilbao

Spotlight: The best I've ever seen

Complete the sentences with your ideas and verbs from the box.

| met   read   been to   seen   eaten |

1 .... is the best film I've ever ....
2 .... is the best book I've ever ....
3 .... is the most expensive restaurant I've ever ....
4 .... is the nicest food I've ever ....
5 .... is the most interesting person I've ever ....

Spelling

Write the comparative and superlative forms of the adjectives.

	Comparative	Superlative
new	....	....
nice	....	....
important	....	....
hot	....	....
wet	....	....
cold	....	....
popular	....	....
angry	....	....

| /ə(r)/ | bigger   greater   smaller   slower   faster   taller   older |
| /ɪst/ | biggest   greatest   smallest   slowest   fastest   tallest   oldest |

EXTENSION 28

Strategies: graded readers

Have you ever read a graded reader in English? Graded readers have easy grammar and vocabulary. There are many series of readers.

Tips for using graded readers
- Don't stop at every new word. Read to the end of the page. You can often guess the meaning of new words.
- Read quickly.
- Highlight difficult words, and come back to them again later.
- There are often pictures. Look at the pictures before you look in a dictionary.
- Use an English-English dictionary first. If you still don't understand, look in a translation dictionary.
- There are sometimes exercises with graded readers.
- There are sometimes audio recordings. You can listen and read. Later, you can listen to the story again without the book.
- Read stories for fun. Don't think of reading as 'more work'.
- Choose from different series. Choose a book that is interesting for you. If it's interesting, you can often read at a higher level.

Spotlight: adjectives

Look at these adjectives.

narrow	small	tiny	short	large	big	tall	high	long
medium	regular	old	cold	expensive	hot	modern		

Which of the adjectives can you use to describe these things?

a building   a person's height   a clothes size
feet   a room   a drink in a fast-food restaurant

A question of pronunciation

The past simple of *read* has the same spelling as the present simple, but the pronunciation is different. The present is *read* /riːd/, but the past is *read* /red/. The past participle is *read* /red/ too. This can be a problem. A few years ago, there was a question in an exam for 11-year-old children. It said, 'Write an essay with the title *Reading*'. Most children in England wrote about their favourite books (*reading* /riːdɪŋ/). But in the town of *Reading* /redɪŋ/, most children wrote an essay about the town.

/iː/	read (present)	immediately	obediently	beat	teach	feel	cheek
/e/	read (past)	said	met	spend	spent	fell	held	felt	best

EXTENSION 29

School subjects

Make three lists about your schooldays.
Put these subjects on the lists, then add others.

| PE (Physical Education) | RE (Religious Education) | Cooking | Music |
| IT (Information Technology) | Science | Politics | Psychology | Typing |

Compulsory subjects (We all had to study them.)	**Optional subjects** (We could study them, but we didn't have to study them.)	**Subjects we couldn't study** (The school didn't teach them.)
Mathematics	Art	Film studies

Ask and answer. (If you are still at school or college, change *Did you have to …?* to *Do you have to …?*)

1. Which subjects did you have to study at secondary school?
2. Could you study other subjects? What were they?
3. Did your parents have to buy the textbooks?
4. Did you have to carry a lot of books to school?
5. Did you have to wear a uniform?
6. Could you call the teachers by their first names?

Connecting

Make sentences with *because*. There is more than correct answer.

They couldn't come to the party		they've got to catch a train.
They had to apologize		they had an exam the next day.
They've got to go now	because	they were busy.
They couldn't drink alcohol		they had to drive home.
They had to stay in and revise		they were late for the lesson.

/ʊ/	good	could	couldn't	would	wouldn't	wood	sugar	cook
/ɒ/	got	college	want	what	washing	popular	robot	promise
/əʊ/	go	cola	won't	don't	wrote	robot	romance	clone	closed

EXTENSION 30

Reading: a joke

Mrs Rigby went to buy some bread. She walked into the baker's and asked for a French stick.
'That's one fifty,' said the baker.
'One fifty! They're much cheaper at the other baker's across the road.'
'So why don't you go to the other baker's?' he said.
'Because they've sold out of French sticks today.'
The baker laughed, 'Well, when they haven't sold out of French sticks, they're cheaper here too.'

Ask and answer.
1. What did she want to buy?
2. Where did she go to buy it?
3. Was it more expensive there, or was it cheaper there?
4. Did the other baker's have any?

Spotlight: apostrophes

You buy newspapers and magazines from a newsagent, at a newsagent's.
A *newsagent* is a person. *Newsagent's* means a newsagent's shop, so it has a possessive *'s*, like *Anna's shop* or *Tom's house*.
A *clothes shop* is an ordinary plural. It sells clothes. There is no apostrophe.

It's often difficult for people to know. On shop signs you will see *hairdressers* (more than one hairdresser works there) or *bakers* (more than one baker works there). Correct English is *I'm going to the hairdressers'* in this situation, but the apostrophe is disappearing from these plurals for shops.

Vocabulary

Add more words to the word map.

Stressed

| to /tuː/ | for /fɔː/ | can /kæn/ | have /hæv/ | has /hæz/ | was /wɒz/ | were /wɜː/ |

Unstressed

| to /tə/ | for /fə/ | can /kən/ | have /həv/ | has /həz/ | was /wəz/ | were /wə/ |

ACTIVITY ONE

Unit three. Student A

How much is it? Ask your partner questions and complete the price list. Make a conversation using the menu.

ACTIVITY TWO

Unit six. Student A

Remember. You can answer with *Yes, I do.* or *No, I don't*.
The facts are about Britain. You can change them for your country.

You are a postman / postwoman.
You work outside.
You wear a uniform.
You work alone.
You work from Monday to Saturday.
You meet people in your job.
You work from 5 a.m. to 11.30 a.m.

ACTIVITY THREE

Unit ten. Student A

You're all at a dinner party. Don't show the other students this information.

The dinner party is at your house. For dinner there is tomato soup, then beefburger and chips, then strawberries and ice-cream.
Tell Students B, C, and D what there is for dinner.

For dinner there is …

ACTIVITY FOUR

Unit seventeen. Student A

Read this information about Jason. Answer Student B's questions.

Newtown defender Jason Dean and pop star Gemma X – romance in the air?

Newtown and England defender Jason Dean was at the Tropical Club in Newtown last night with pop star Gemma X. Gemma (age 19) was number two in the Top-20 last month. They were at the club until 3 a.m. Jason was with four other Newtown players, and they were very noisy! Our photographer was outside the club, and Gemma was in Jason's Ferrari in this photograph.

ACTIVITY FIVE

Unit fourteen. Student A

Find these in your picture.
the grandmother, the father, the mother, the son, the daughter, the dog

Answer Student B's questions about your picture.

Student B's picture has got the same people. Ask about them.
What is the grandmother doing?

ACTIVITY SIX

Unit sixteen. Student A

This is your calendar. Arrange a meeting with Students B and C. Don't show them your calendar.

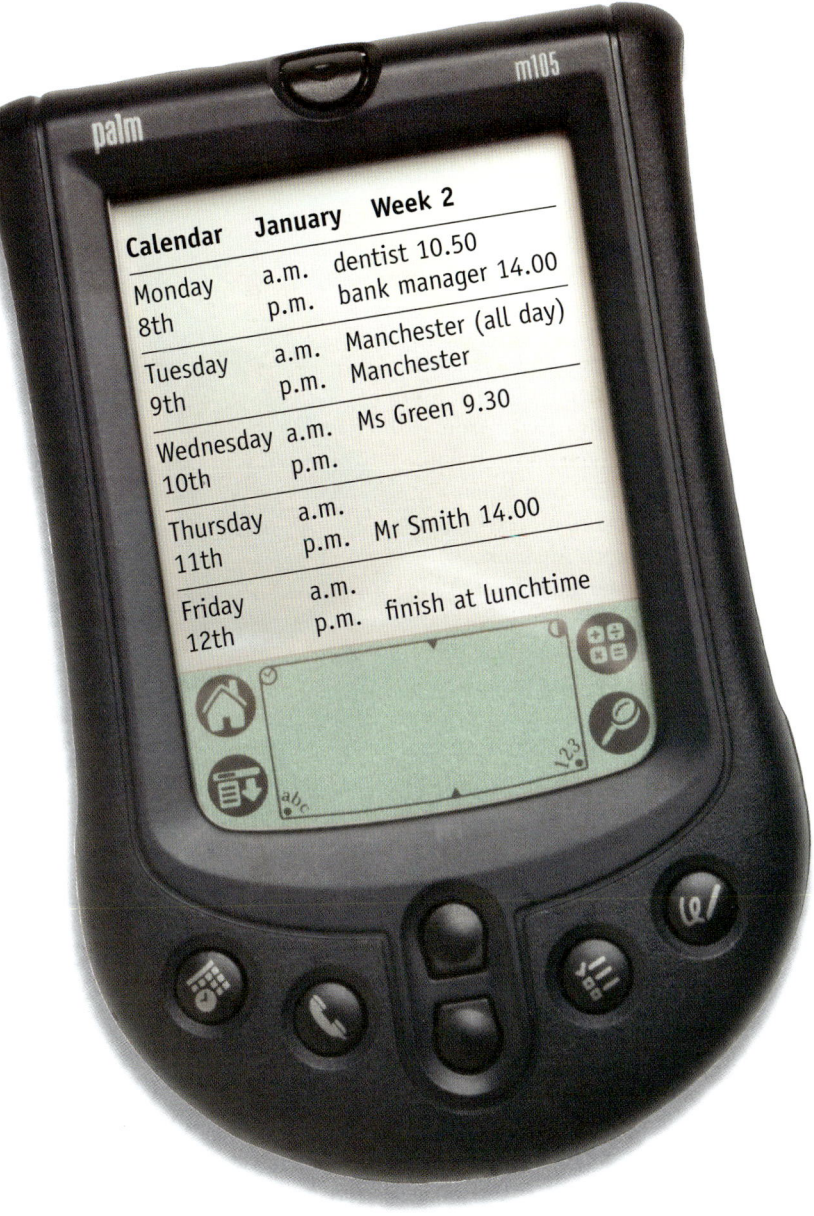

Calendar	January	Week 2
Monday 8th	a.m.	dentist 10.50
	p.m.	bank manager 14.00
Tuesday 9th	a.m.	Manchester (all day)
	p.m.	Manchester
Wednesday 10th	a.m.	Ms Green 9.30
	p.m.	
Thursday 11th	a.m.	
	p.m.	Mr Smith 14.00
Friday 12th	a.m.	
	p.m.	finish at lunchtime

ACTIVITY SEVEN

Unit nineteen. Student A

**Read the information about Robin Taylor.
Student B has information about his brother, Robert Campbell, for the same years.**

1 **Ask Student B about the years.**
    ▶ What happened in 1959?
    ◀ Mrs and Mrs Campbell adopted him. They called him Robert.

2 **Then check the information.**
    ▶ When did Mr and Mrs Campbell adopt him?
    ◀ They adopted him in 1959.
    ▶ What did they call him?
    ◀ They called him Robert.

27th December 1958 He was born in Birmingham at 9.15.
1959 Mr and Mrs Taylor from Birmingham adopted him. They called him Robin.
1960 The Taylors moved to Perth in Western Australia.
1964 Robin started school. All his friends called him Rob.
1971 Robin played football for his school football team.
1974 Robin met his first girlfriend.
1977 Robin went to university. He studied physics. He wanted to be an astronaut.
1981 Robin got his first job. He was a physics teacher.
1985 He met Linda. She was a nurse. Linda's parents were Scottish.
1986 He married Linda.
1989 His twin sons, Mark and Martin, were born.
1993 His daughter, Debbie, was born.
2001 He moved to a new house.
2003 Robin bought a new car. It was a blue Ford.

ACTIVITY EIGHT

Unit twenty-seven. Student A

The greatest rock album of all time.
Rock critics and surveys have chosen The Beatles' 'Sergeant Pepper's Lonely Heart's Club Band' more than any other album. It's not in the Top-20 for sales. The Beatles are the best-selling group of all time. Elvis Presley is the best-selling male artist. Madonna is the best-selling female artist.

The fastest-selling record ever.
Elton John, 'Candle in The Wind' (1997). This was a tribute to Diana, Princess of Wales. The words are different from the original 1973 recording (which was about Marilyn Monroe).

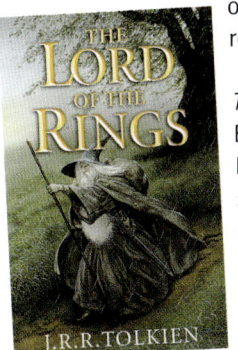

The best book of the 20th century.
British readers voted J.R.R. Tolkien's 'The Lord of The Rings' the best book of the 20th century in a very large survey done by newspapers and bookshops. It won easily. This was before the films.

The largest planet in our solar system.
Jupiter. It is 317 times the mass of the Earth.

The worst natural disaster of the 20th century.
Earthquake in Tang-shan, China, 28th July 1976. 242, 419 people died.

The most popular film of the 20th century.
'Gone With The Wind' (1939) is first, because 208 million people saw it in the first year. 'Star Wars' is second (198 million). 'Titanic' is fifth (124 million). But in money for tickets, 'Titanic' is first.

The most expensive film of the 20th century.
'Titanic' (250 million dollars), then 'Waterworld' (175 million dollars). 'Cleopatra' cost 44 million dollars in 1963, and in modern money it's the most expensive.

The most successful international football team.
Brazil has won most World Cups (five) at the time of writing.

ACTIVITY NINE

Unit ten. Student B

You're all at a dinner party.
Don't show the other students this information.

The dinner party is at Student A's house.
You are allergic to tomatoes and strawberries. You like chips very much.
You can eat beef, but you're worried about British beef.

ACTIVITY TEN

Unit twenty-three. Student A

1 It's Saturday. Jack and Anna are on holiday in Canada.
   They're in Winnipeg tonight.

   Answer Student B's questions.

   ITINERARY
   Canadian Highlights: 7 days by air

Tuesday	Arrive Montreal
Wednesday	Montreal
Thursday	Ottawa
Friday	Toronto
Saturday	Winnipeg
Sunday	Calgary
Monday	Vancouver
Tuesday	Depart Vancouver

2 Paula is on holiday in Australia.

   Ask Student B questions and complete her itinerary. Begin:
   Where is she? Which day is it?

   ITINERARY
   Australian Adventure: 7 days by air

   Monday
   Tuesday
   Wednesday
   Thursday
   Friday
   Saturday
   Sunday
   Monday

ACTIVITY ELEVEN

Unit twenty-eight

Put your words in the correct places, e.g. (1) is a woman's first name.

(1).................. went to (2) .... for her holiday. She stayed there for a week. On the fifth evening she went to a (3).................. . The waiter was very polite and friendly. His name was (4).................. . He had (5).................. hair. She liked him. At the end of the evening, he said, 'Would you like to meet me tomorrow? I'll take you to see the (6).................. .'
'OK,' she said immediately. 'What time?'
'I'll meet you at seven o'clock.'
'Where?' she said.
'Outside the (7).................. .'
(1).................. arrived at five to seven. She waited for (8).................. , but he didn't come. She felt (9).................. .
On her last morning, she was outside her hotel. She saw (4).................. again. He looked very (10).................. . Her heart beat loudly.

'Where were you?' she said. 'I waited for (8).................. .'
He looked down. She held her breath, and waited for his answer.
'I waited for (8).................. too,' he said. 'But you didn't come.'
'I was there at five to seven,' she said.
'It's a pity,' he said. 'It was a beautiful morning.'
'Morning?' she said. 'I was there at seven o'clock in the evening.'
'Oh, no!' he said. 'Well, we can go to the (6).................. another time. Perhaps we can meet on (11).................. .'
'It's my last day,' she said. 'My plane leaves at (12).................. .'
A tear fell down his cheek, 'We'll never meet again,' he said.
She hugged him. 'I'm so sorry,' she said quietly. 'But give me your address. I'll write to you, I promise.'

Read your story to another student.
Who wrote the funniest story?

ACTIVITY TWELVE

Unit twenty-nine

Women have to cover their heads in religious buildings. They can't wear short skirts.
This is true in many countries. It's true in Catholic churches, Muslim mosques, and Buddhist temples.

You can't drink alcohol until you're twenty-one. Young people have to show ID-cards in restaurants and bars.
True in the USA.

You have to take off your shoes in private homes.
True in most of Asia and the Middle-East. It's not usual in Europe or America.

Motorcyclists have to wear crash helmets, but they can't wear them in petrol stations or banks.
True in Britain. Most petrol stations have signs, 'Motorcyclists please remove your helmets.' This is because robbers sometimes wear helmets.

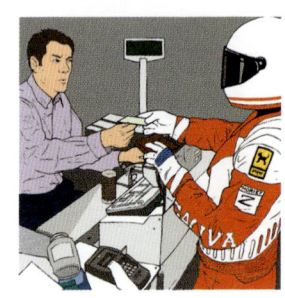

You don't have to show passports when travelling between countries.
True in most European Union countries (but not Britain, at the time of writing). You show your passport in the first EU country that you arrive in.

You have to give your seat to monks on buses and trains.
True in Thailand, and in other Buddhist countries. In France you have to give your seat to ex-soldiers who were injured in wars. In Britain, seats near the door on buses are reserved for mothers with young children and disabled people.

ACTIVITY THIRTEEN

Unit three. Student B

How much is it? Ask your partner questions and complete the price list. Make a conversation with the menu.

Quick-Food
PRICE LIST   EAT IN OR TAKE OUT

hamburger
......

cheeseburger
3.40

hot dog
......

pizza
......

spaghetti bolognese .
3.80

chocolate cake
1.30

cola:
regular ......
large 1.60

milk:
regular 1.15
large ......

coffee:
cappuccino 1.85
espresso ......

pot of tea
2.10

orange juice
......

ice-cream: 1.75
vanilla, chocolate
or strawberry

ACTIVITY FOURTEEN

Unit six. Student B

Remember. You can answer with *Yes, I do.* or *No, I don't.*
The facts are about Britain. You can change them for your country.

You are a flight attendant.
You work on an aeroplane.
You wear a uniform.
You work with food.
You meet people in your job.
You don't work from Monday to Saturday.
You don't work from nine to five.
You work three or four days a week.
You travel.

ACTIVITY FIFTEEN

Unit ten. Student C

You're all at a dinner party.
Don't show the other students this information.

The dinner party is at Student A's house.
You can eat fruit, salad, and fish.
You can eat strawberries, but you don't like them.

ACTIVITY SIXTEEN

Unit seventeen. Student B

Student A has got information about Jason.
Ask Student A questions.
1. Where was Jason last night?
2. Who was he with?
3. Was he at the club at 2.30 a.m.?
4. Was he at the club at 3.30 a.m.?
5. Were there other Newtown players at the club?
6. How many were there?
7. Where was the photographer?
8. Who was in Jason's car?

ACTIVITY SEVENTEEN

Unit fourteen. Student B

Find these in your picture.
the grandmother, the father, the mother, the son, the daughter, the dog

Student A's picture has got the same people. Ask about them.
What is the grandmother doing?

Then answer Student A's questions about your picture.

ACTIVITY EIGHTEEN

Unit sixteen. Student B

This is your calendar. Arrange a meeting with Students A and C. Don't show them your calendar.

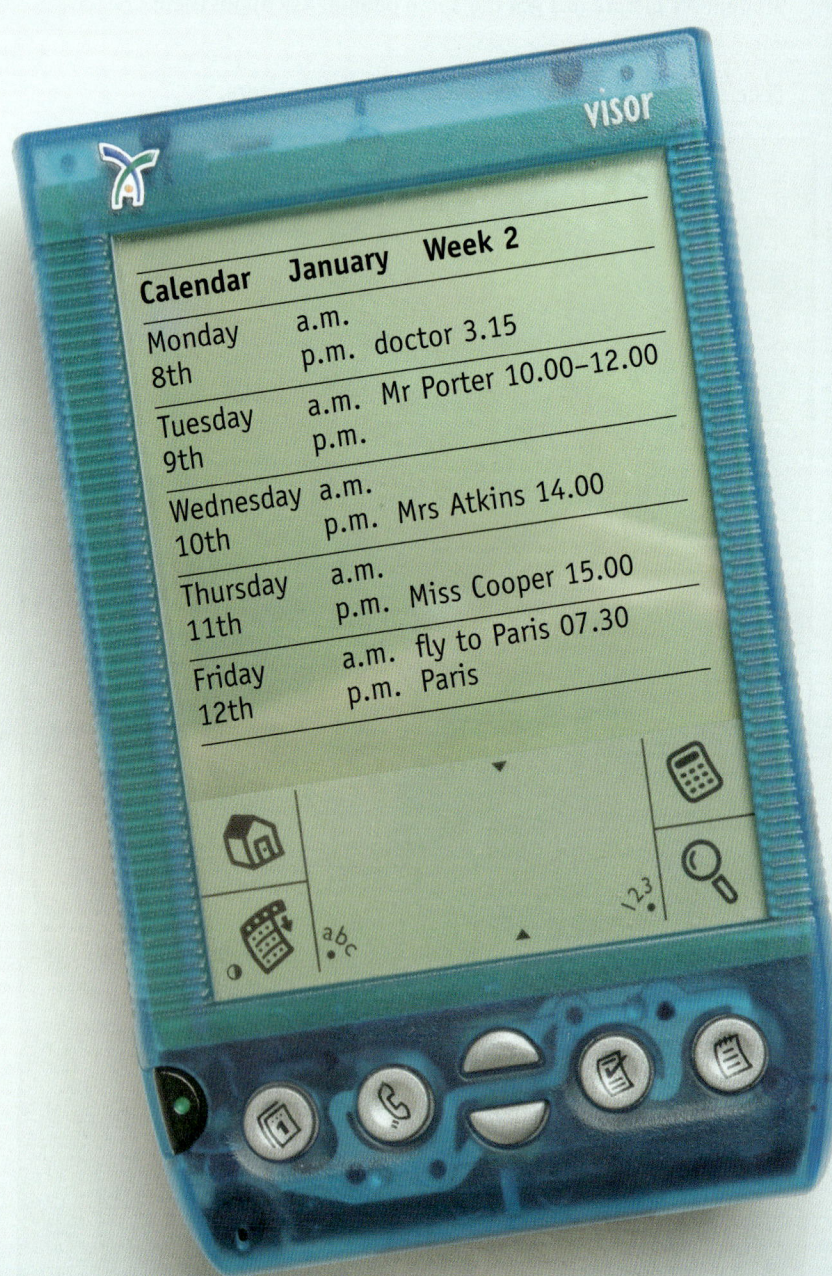

Calendar	January	Week 2
Monday 8th	a.m.	
	p.m. doctor 3.15	
Tuesday 9th	a.m. Mr Porter 10.00–12.00	
	p.m.	
Wednesday 10th	a.m.	
	p.m. Mrs Atkins 14.00	
Thursday 11th	a.m.	
	p.m. Miss Cooper 15.00	
Friday 12th	a.m. fly to Paris 07.30	
	p.m. Paris	

ACTIVITY NINETEEN

Unit nineteen. Student B

**Read the information about Robert Campbell.
Student A has information about his brother, Robin Taylor, for the same years.**

1 **Ask Student A about the years.**
   ▶ What happened in 1959?
   ◀ Mr and Mrs Taylor adopted him. They called him Robin.

2 **Then check the information.**
   ▶ When did Mr and Mrs Taylor adopt him?
   ◀ They adopted him in 1959.
   ▶ What did they call him?
   ◀ They called him Robin.

27th December 1958 He was born in Birmingham at 9.35.
1959 Mr and Mrs Campbell adopted him. Mr Campbell had a job in Birmingham. They called him Robert.
1963 The Campbells moved back to their home town, Perth in Scotland.
1964 Robert started school. All his friends called him Rob.
1971 Robert played football for his school football team.
1974 Robert met his first girlfriend.
1977 Robert went to university. He studied chemistry. He wanted to be an astronaut.
1981 Robert got his first job. He was a chemistry teacher.
1985 He met Maggie. She was a nurse. Maggie's parents were Scottish.
1986 He married Maggie.
1989 His twin daughters, Deborah and Dawn, were born.
1993 His son, Martin, was born.
2001 He moved to a new house.
2003 Robert bought a new car. It was a blue Ford.

ACTIVITY TWENTY

Unit ten. Student D

You're all at a dinner party.
Don't show the other students this information.

The dinner party is at Student A's house.
You are a vegetarian. You can't eat meat or fish. You don't like soup.

ACTIVITY TWENTY-ONE

Unit twenty-three. Student B

1 Jack and Anna are on holiday in Canada. Ask Student A questions and complete their itinerary. Begin:
   Where are they? Which day is it?

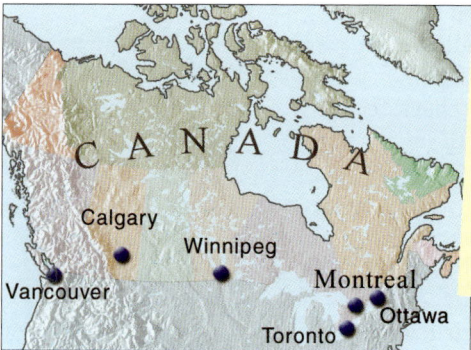

ITINERARY
Canadian Highlights: 7 days by air
Tuesday
Wednesday
Thursday
Friday
Saturday
Sunday
Monday
Tuesday

2 Paula is on holiday in Australia. She's in Darwin tonight.
   Answer Student A's questions.

ITINERARY
Australian Adventure: 7 days by air

Monday	Arrive Perth
Tuesday	Perth
Wednesday	Alice Springs
Thursday	Darwin
Friday	Brisbane
Saturday	Sydney
Sunday	Melbourne
Monday	Depart Melbourne

ACTIVITY TWENTY-TWO

Unit sixteen. Student C

This is your calendar. Arrange a meeting with Students A and B. Don't show them your calendar.

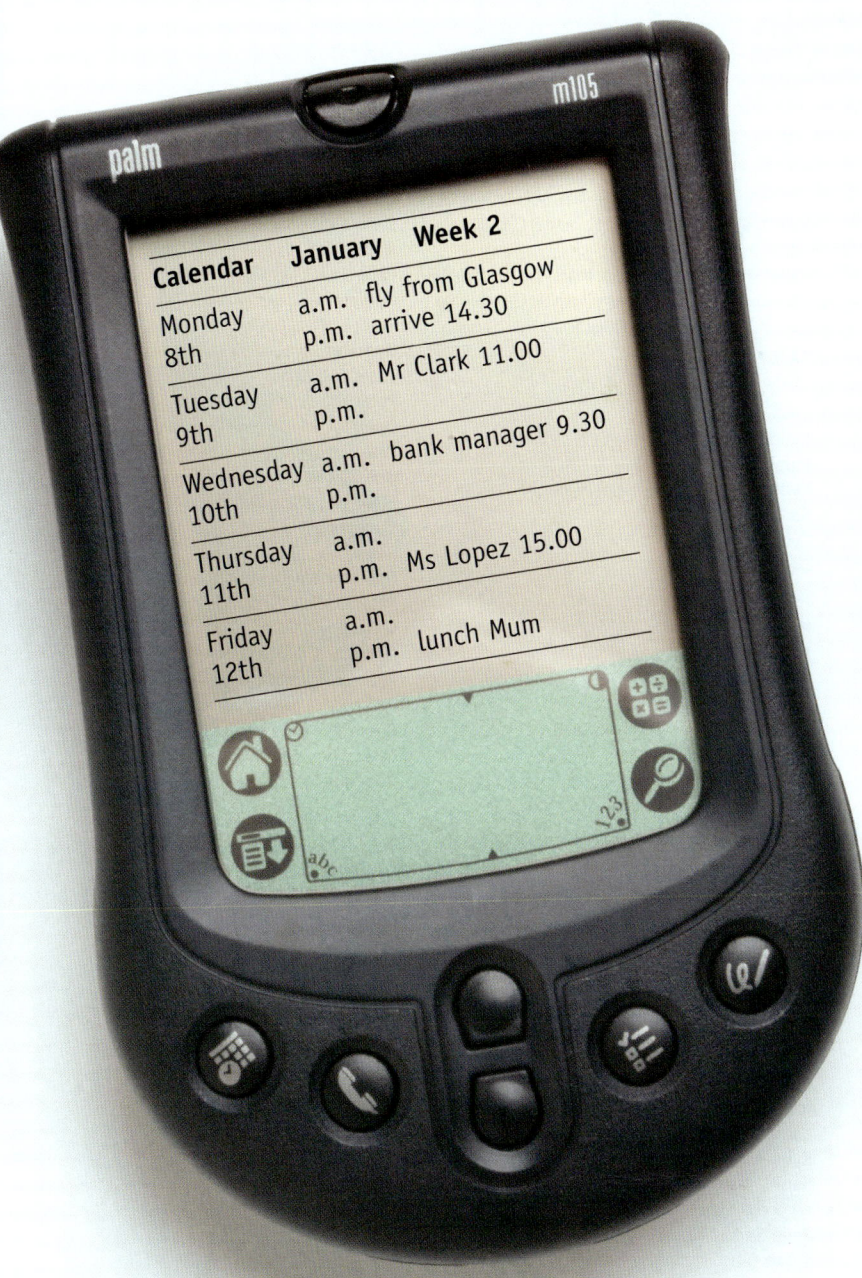

Calendar	January	Week 2
Monday 8th	a.m.	fly from Glasgow
	p.m.	arrive 14.30
Tuesday 9th	a.m.	Mr Clark 11.00
	p.m.	
Wednesday 10th	a.m.	bank manager 9.30
	p.m.	
Thursday 11th	a.m.	
	p.m.	Ms Lopez 15.00
Friday 12th	a.m.	
	p.m.	lunch Mum

TRANSCRIPT

(1.06)

Kylie Welcome to the fitness class. I'm Kylie Winton, and I'm your teacher. Hi! OK, What's your name?
Josh Josh Floyd.
Kylie Can you spell Floyd, please?
Josh Sure. F-L-O-Y-D. Floyd.
Kylie Thank you, Mr Floyd.
Josh Please, call me Josh.
Kylie OK, thanks, Josh.

(1.07)

Kylie Great. What's your name?
Sam McQueen. Sam McQueen.
Kylie Can you spell that, Mr McQueen?
Sam Yes, Capital M, small C, capital Q-U-double E-N.
Kylie Sorry, can you repeat that?
Sam Yes, Capital M, small C, capital Q-U-double E-N. McQueen. Sam McQueen.
Kylie Can I call you Sam?
Sam Yes, no problem.

(1.08)

Kylie And what's your name?
Sarah Sarah.
Kylie And your family name, Sarah?
Sarah Baxter.
Kylie Baxter. Is that B-A-X-T-E-R?
Sarah That's right.

(1.09)

Kylie Good. Next?
Fiona My name's Fiona. Fiona Stewart.
Kylie Stewart. Is that S-T-E-W-A-R-T or S-T-U-A-R-T?
Fiona S-T-E-W-A-R-T. You can call me Fiona.
Kylie Thanks, Fiona.

(1.10)

Kylie Hi. Your name?
Patrick Patrick Neill.
Kylie How do you spell 'Neill'?
Patrick N-E-I-double L.
Kylie Two l's at the end?
Patrick Right.
Kylie Thanks, Patrick.
Patrick My friends call me Pat.
Kylie OK, Pat.

(1.12)

Kylie What's your phone number, Josh?
Josh O two seven, five four three, eight O double nine.
Kylie What's your telephone number, Sam?
Sam My number's O two O, one double three, six O eight four.
Kylie Sarah? What's your number?
Sarah O two eight, three one nine, double four seven six.

Kylie What's your phone number, Fiona?
Fiona My mobile phone's O seven three seven two, nine six one, eight double O.
Kylie Pat?
Patrick My phone number's O eight seven O, three two one, nine six four.

(1.22)

Operator Thank you for your order. Are you paying by Visa or MasterCard?
Peter Visa.
Operator And what's your credit card number?
Peter Double O nine seven, eight six four one, five six two eight, three one double six.
Operator So that's double O nine seven, eight six four one, five six two eight, three one double six?
Peter That's right.
Operator And expiry date?
Peter Twelve, O nine.
Operator For security reasons, can I ask you some questions?
Peter OK. No problem.
Operator What's your date of birth?
Peter Eighteen, eight, eighty.
Operator What's your address?
Peter Flat 50, 15 West Street, Camford.
Operator What's your post code?
Peter CH14 4EI
Operator What's your phone number?
Peter O eight seven O, three two double five seven one.
Operator Thank you. Here's your order reference number.
Peter OK.
Operator Reference number 19-16-90-40-60-17.
Peter Sorry, can you repeat that?
Operator Yes. 19-16-90-40-60-17.

(1.23)

A
Customer A chocolate donut, please.
Server One fifty.
B
Customer A croissant please.
Server With butter 'n' jam?
Customer Please.
Server Two fifteen, please.
C
Customer A slice of pizza, please.
Server Two sixty-five.
D
Customer An American muffin, please.
Server Chocolate or blueberry?
Customer Blueberry.
Server One seventy-five.

TRANSCRIPT

E
Customer How much is a tuna sandwich?
Server Three pounds.
F
Customer An espresso, please.
Server Single or double?
Customer Er, double, please.
Server That's one ninety.

 1.27

Server Can I help you?
Customer Yes, an egg and bacon sandwich, please.
Server Anything else?
Customer Yes, a chocolate donut.
Server Anything to drink?
Customer Yes, please. A lemonade.
Server Regular or large?
Customer Large.
Server That's six fifty.
Customer Thank you.
Server You're welcome.

 1.28

Father Right. Lunchtime. Let's have something to eat. Andrew, are you hungry?
Son Yeah. Pizza for me.
Father How about a sandwich?
Son No. Pizza. It's my favourite. With ketchup.
Father Ketchup? On a pizza?
Son Yeah, Dad, ketchup. And a chocolate donut.
Daughter Ergh.
Father Anything to drink?
Son A cola.
Father OK. And for you, Victoria?
Daughter An orange juice.
Father Anything to eat?
Daughter No, Dad. I'm on a diet!
Father How about an egg and bacon sandwich?
Daughter Dad! I'm vegetarian!
Father Oh, yes, sorry. How about a cheese and tomato sandwich?
Daughter No, thanks. Just an orange juice.
Father OK.

1.29

Server Can I help you?
Father Please. Um, a slice of pizza …
Son With ketchup.
Father With ketchup.
Server Ketchup's over there. On the table.
Father OK. And a chocolate donut, and an almond Danish pastry.
Server Anything to drink?
Father Yes, a cola, and …
Server Regular or large cola?
Father Regular.
Son Large.
Father OK, large. And an orange juice, and a tea.
Server A cup or a pot?
Father A pot for one.
Server There you go. Anything else?
Father No. That's all. How much is that altogether?
Server Eleven eighty, please.
Father Thank you.
Server You're welcome.

 1.31

Guide Right … this way, please. Ah, yes, yes. This is the Mona Lisa, I think. And it's by Leonardo … um … Leonardo diCaprio, the famous, um, Spanish artist. It's a very famous painting. Very. And it's old.
Tourist How old is it?
Guide Oh, very old. And it…
Tourist How old is it exactly?
Guide Ooh, a hundred … no, two hundred years old. She's beautiful, and her smile is … um, very nice.

1.43

1 Have you got a job?
2 Do you work in an office?
3 Are you a receptionist?
4 Do you work in a big city?
5 Do you work at weekends?

1.44

Man I haven't got a job at the moment. I'm unemployed.
Woman I haven't got a job. I've got two small children at home. I'm a full-time mother.
Retired man I'm 66. I haven't got a job. I'm retired.
Student I haven't got a job. I'm at university. I'm a student.

 1.46

Q Good evening! We've got four panellists in the studio tonight. First, the TV Chef, Oliver James …
OJ Hi.
Q And sitting next to him, from the TV soap 'Westenders', we've got Charlene Moult.
CM Hello.
Q From Oxford University, Dr Jennifer Castle.
JC Good evening.
Q And finally, the politician, Lord Stanley Gilbert.
Lord S A very good evening to you all.
Q And here's our first contestant, Mr Brian Harding from Barnet. Sit down, Mr Harding.
Mr H Thank you.
Q Right. The first question. Oliver …

TRANSCRIPT

OJ Oh, right. Hi. Er, do you work in an office?
Mr H No, I don't.
CM Hello, Brian. Um, do you work in a hospital?
Mr H No.
JC Do you work inside?
Mr H No, I don't.
Lord S So, do you work outside?
Mr H Yes, I do.
Lord S Do you work in the country?
Mr H No, I don't.
OJ Do you wear a uniform?
Mr H Well, I wear special clothes, yes.
OJ Are you a policeman?
Mr H No, I'm not.
CM Have you got any qualifications for your job?
Mr H Yes, I have.
CM Have you got a university degree?
Mr H No, I haven't.
JC Do women do your job?
Mr H Uh, well, yes, they do.
JC Ah, Do many women do your job?
Mr H No, they don't.
Q That's seven 'no' answers.
Lord S Do you travel in your job?
Mr H Yes, I do.
Lord S Do you work from Monday to Friday?
Mr H No, I don't!
Q Eight 'no' answers.
OJ Do you work at weekends?
JC We know that, Oliver.
OJ Do we?
JC He doesn't work from Monday to Friday.
OJ Oh, right, yes. Um, do you work on Saturday?
Mr H Yes, I do.
OJ A guess ... are you a footballer?
Mr H No, I'm not.
Q That's nine.
CM Oh, it's me! Do you work in sport?
Mr H Yes, I do.
CM Oh. What sport?
Q You can't ask that.
CM Oh. And it's not football?
Q He isn't a footballer.
CM Do you play tennis?
Mr H No, I don't.
Q That's ten 'no' answers!

Stop the audio. What does he do? Can you guess?

(1.47)
Q OK, Brian. Tell them. What do you do?
Mr H I'm a football referee.

(1.48)
Operator Thank you for your order. Can I have your address?
Matt Yes. It's 32, Kinson Road, Northbourne, Bournemouth, Dorset.
Operator 32 Kinson Road ... How do you spell Bournemouth?
Matt B-O-U-R-N-E-M-O-U-T-H.
Operator And your post code?
Matt It's BH7 8RD.
Operator BH7 8RD ... 8, R for radio, D for Delta?
Matt That's right.
Operator Is there a contact number?
Matt Yes, it's 0 one two 0 two, one three double 8 double 7.
Operator Have you got an e-mail address?
Matt Yes. It's M Jackson at fastnet dot co dot UK.
Operator M Jackson? Is there a dot after the M?
Matt No, there isn't. Just M Jackson, as one word.

(1.49)
Diane Smith Incorporated.
Tony Hi, Diane?
Diane Yes, speaking.
Tony It's Tony, from England.
Diane Oh, hi, Tony.
Tony Hi. Diane, I've got a birthday card for you, and I haven't got your new home address.
Diane Oh, OK. It's Apartment fifty.
Tony Fifteen?
Diane No, fifty. Two seven one five Eglinton Avenue ... that's E-G-L-I-N-T-O-N North York, Toronto, Ontario M3P 4H9.
Tony Great.
Diane Oh, Tony ...
Tony Yes?
Diane My home phone number's one 0 two, eight three five 0.
Tony What's the Toronto area code?
Diane 416.
Tony And what's your e-mail address?
Diane diane dot conway at sympatico dot C-A.
Tony C-O? Co?
Diane No, C-A ... for Canada.

(1.53)
A Excuse me ...
Clerk Yes?
A What time does the New York flight arrive?
Clerk VS eighteen from Newark? That arrives at twenty hundred.
A No, not Newark. New York.
Clerk Which one? There are two.
A The American Airlines flight.
Clerk That arrives at twenty twenty.
A Is it on time?
Clerk Yes, it is.

TRANSCRIPT

1.56

A Have you got everything?
B Yes, it's all here.
A Passports?
B Yes.
A Train tickets?
B Of course. Don't worry.
A Have we got seat reservations?
B Yes. Car 4. Seats B-15 and B-16.
A What about the hotel vouchers?
B They're in my bag.
A Oh. What about money?
B You've got it.
A Have I?
B Yes. It's in your bag.
A Oh, yes. Here it is. Oh, we haven't got anything to read.
B It's OK. I've got some magazines.
A What about food? We can get some sandwiches.
B No, there's a buffet on the train.

1.57

A What time is it?
B A quarter past nine.
A What time does our train leave?
B Nine twenty-seven.
Announcer The nine twenty-seven service to Disneyland Paris is now boarding at platform two.
A Ooh. Are there any toilets here?
B Yes, there are. But you haven't got time. The train's boarding now.
A We've got twelve minutes …
B It's OK. There are toilets on the train.
A Are you sure?
B Yes, I'm sure.
Announcer Would all passengers for train number 9074 to Disneyland Paris go immediately to platform two.
B Come on. Let's go.

1.60

A I come here by underground, then I walk from the station.
B Just before nine. I start work at nine.
C Yes, I have. It's an old Ford Focus.
D About twenty minutes on the train. Then it's a two-minute walk.
E I leave just after 8.20. My train leaves at 8.30. They're very busy at that time of the day.

1.61

Woman Be careful! Don't go in there!
Child Why not?
Woman It's dangerous. That's why!

1.62

Stop! Don't walk! The light's on red.

1.63

Woman Look! You can see the sea! What a lovely view …
Man Please! Be careful … don't go near the edge. The cliffs aren't safe.

1.64

Cop Hey! Bud, get off that bike.
Man What?
Cop Don't ride on the sidewalk, OK?

1.65

Don't go near the railway line. There's a train coming. I can hear it.

1.66

Old lady Come on, Rover, that's a good boy … this way …
Inspector Excuse me, madam. Please don't take your dog on the beach.
Old lady Oh, I'm sorry.

1.69

OK, be quiet, please! Let's have the tall ones in the back row. Can I have number three, number six, number eleven … and the goalkeeper, number one. Stand behind the chairs. Good. Mmm. Number three on the left … no, my left. Then six, then the goalkeeper, and number eleven on my right. Number six? You're between number three and the goalkeeper. That's it.

Now the middle row. Number ten, number five, number two, and number eight. Number ten on the left. Then five, then two. Sit on the chairs. No, number eight. Don't sit there. Sit on the right. No, not your right. Sit on my right. Thank you.

The front row. Where's the captain? Put your hand up. Right, you're number nine. OK, kneel in the middle, and hold the cup. Fine. Number seven? Kneel next to the captain. On my right. On my right. OK. And number four, kneel on the left. Yes, there. Hmm. Good. Where's the manager? Stand next to number three.

Goalkeeper, take off your cap, please. Oh, dear. No, put it on again. Umm. Number four, hold the mascot. No, be quiet, please. Don't laugh. And number seven, hold the football.

Number eleven. Don't look over there. Look at me. And number five, don't look at him. Thank you. And don't chew gum, number six. Take it out. No, don't put it there. OK, ready? Smile! Say 'cheese'! Thank you.

1.70

Back row, from left to right: three, six, one, eleven. Middle row, from left to right: ten, five, two, eight. Front row, from left to right: four,

TRANSCRIPT

nine, seven.

(1.73)
Aunt Hello, David. How are you, dear?
David Very well, thank you. Er, this is Vicki.
Aunt Oh, hello, Victoria.
Vicki Hello.
Aunt Ugh ... Is that your dog?
David Yes, it's ...
Aunt Oh, David! You know all about my allergies! I can't go near a dog! Take it away!

(1.74)
Vicki Lunch is in the garden.
Aunt Outside? I can't sit outside.
Vicki But it's a lovely day.
Aunt Not for me. I've got hay fever.
Vicki Oh, OK. We can go into the dining room. This way ...
Aunt There are flowers on the table.
Vicki Yes, they're roses from our garden.
Aunt Please take them away. I'm very allergic to roses.

(1.75)
Vicki There you are ... it's a cheese salad.
Aunt Oh, dear.
Vicki Is there something wrong?
Aunt Well, yes. I can't eat cheese. I'm allergic to it, you see.
Vicki I'm sorry ...
Aunt And I can't eat potatoes. I'm on a diet.
Vicki Well, you can have some quiche. Pass me your plate.
Aunt Is that meat?
Vicki Where?
Aunt There! On the quiche!
Vicki Yes, it's just a little bit of bacon.
Aunt I can't eat that! I'm a vegetarian.

(1.76)
David What can you have, Aunt Jemima?
Aunt Well, I can't eat bread. Or nuts. I can't drink tea or coffee. And I can't wear nylon. I can't ...
David We've got some ice-cream in the fridge. Can you eat ice-cream?
Aunt Ice-cream? Yes, I can eat that. What flavour is it?
David Chocolate.
Aunt Oh, no! I can't.
David Are you allergic to chocolate, too?
Aunt No, I'm not. But I don't like it.

(1.77)
Mark I'm a student and I don't like cooking. My fridge is pretty disgusting! There are some pizzas ...yeah, five pizzas. They're all cheese and tomato. That's my favourite. And there's some beer. Uh, one, two, three ... yeah, there are five cans of beer. I've got some sausages. Mmm. They're too old. I can't eat those ... And some milk. Yeah, that's OK.

(1.78)
Joan Well, I'm retired. I live on my own now. Just me and my cat. In my fridge there's some cat food for Tibby. She doesn't eat very much nowadays. She's fourteen, you know. There are some potatoes. They're from yesterday's dinner. Um, there are some sardines on a plate, and they're for my dinner tonight. And I've got some peas for tonight as well.

(1.79)
James I've got a very large American refrigerator. I live on my own, but I have friends to dinner every weekend. So I've got some champagne. There's some cheese. It's French cheese, Camembert. I buy it from a specialist cheese shop in London. It's very expensive. There's some beef. Fillet steak, of course. And some fresh strawberries. They're imported. They come from California.

(1.80)
Helen I'm a vegetarian, actually. I don't eat meat or fish. I've got some yoghurt. I have yoghurt for breakfast because it's very good for you. And there's some salad. I eat a lot of salad. I've got some beans, and some mineral water. That's it!

(1.89)
Announcer Would passengers for Flight 372 go immediately to Gate 4 where this flight is now boarding.
Server Next, please. How may I help you?
Man I'd like a coffee, please.
Server What kind?
Man What kind have you got?
Server We have cappuccino, espresso, latte, Americano, macchiato ...
Man Just normal coffee. I'm in a hurry.
Server So you want Americano?
Man If that's normal coffee, yes.
Server Hot coffee or iced coffee?
Man Normal. Hot.
Server Would you like Colombian, Brazilian, Mexican, Kenyan, Blue Mountain, Indonesian Special Blend ...
Man It doesn't matter.
Server Colombian?
Man OK.
Announcer This is the final call for passengers on Flight 372. Please report to the gate immediately.
Server Regular or decaf?

TRANSCRIPT

Man Regular. Look, my plane leaves in …
Server Do you want black or white coffee?
Man White.
Server Would you like cream, milk or half and half with that?
Man What's half and half?
Server That's half milk and half cream.
Man Milk.
Server Full-fat milk, half-fat milk or low-fat milk?
Man Just milk. I'd like ordinary milk.
Server OK. Full-fat milk. Would you like sugar?
Man Yes, please. Look, I'm really in a hurry …
Server Brown sugar, white sugar, or low-calorie sweetener?
Man It really doesn't matter. Oh, brown sugar.
Server What size?
Man Just a cup.
Server Would you like a small cup, a regular cup, a large cup or an extra large cup?
Man Large. No, small.
Server Is that to drink here or to take out?
Man To drink here. Now. My plane leaves in two minutes …
Server Would you like a muffin with that? We have chocolate, blueberry, cinnamon and apple, raisin …
Man No. Just the coffee.
Announcer Flight 372 to San Diego is now closing at Gate 4.
Man Sorry. Forget the coffee. I haven't got time.
Server OK.

(1.96)
Conversation 1
Assistant May I help you?
Customer No, thank you. I'm just looking.
Conversation 2
Assistant Can I help you?
Customer Yes. I'm looking for the men's department.
Assistant It's on the second floor.

(1.98)
Assistant Are you waiting?
Customer Er, yes. Yes. I'm looking for a song.
Assistant What's the title?
Customer I don't know. But it's on the radio.
Assistant I see. Who's the artist?
Customer I don't know. It's an old song.
Assistant Uh, do you know the words?
Customer Um, yes … it's … uh … 'I'm walking …' somewhere …
Assistant Can you sing it?
Customer What? In here?
Assistant Yes.
Customer 'I'm walking to New Orleans…'
Assistant No, I don't know it.
Customer He's American.
Assistant Ah.
Customer He's very good.
Assistant Mmm. Let me check the computer. I … I'm … I'm walking … No … W … walking … Yes, here it is. 'Walking to New Orleans' by Fats Domino.
Customer Great! That's it! Have you got it?
Assistant No, we haven't. But we can order it.
Customer OK. How much is it?
Assistant It's a greatest hits CD. It's fourteen ninety-nine.
Customer That's fine.

(2.02)
Martin Trimble is in his office. It's eleven o'clock at night and his computer isn't working. He's phoning his boss at home.
T (whispers) Hello? This is Tiffany.
M Hello. Can I speak to your father, please?
T No.
M Can I speak to your mother, then?
T No.
M How old are you, Tiffany?
T I'm four.
M Is there anyone else there?
T Yes. A policewoman.
M Really? What's she doing?
T She's talking to Mummy and Daddy … and to the firefighters.
M The firefighters?
T Yes. There are lots and lots of policemen and policewomen, and lots and lots of firefighters. And a big, red fire engine!
M Oh, dear. What are you doing now, Tiffany?
T I'm hiding under the bed in Mummy and Daddy's room.
M What's that noise?
T It's a police helicopter. It's landing in the garden.

(2.03)
M Why are they all there? What's happening?
T They're all looking for me!

(2.16)
H OK. Let's arrange the next meeting. How about Monday the 8th in the afternoon? Chelsea?
C Yeah. That's good for me.
H Adam?
A Um, Monday the 8th? No, sorry, Harry, I can't. I'm meeting my bank manager at two thirty.
H Right. What about Thursday the 11th?
C In the morning?
H Yes.
C I'm free.
A No, sorry, I can't do Thursday. I'm going to Liverpool.

TRANSCRIPT

H Right. Friday the 12th?
C Yep.
A No … I've got two appointments on the 12th.
H Phew. The 15th? Lunchtime?
A No, sorry. I'm seeing my girlfriend then.
H Can't you change it?
A It's her birthday. I'm taking her to lunch.
H Well, we can't wait too long. When's good for you, Adam?
A Tomorrow? Ten o'clock?
H Fine for me.
C Sorry. I'm … No, no. It doesn't matter. I can change it.
H Great. Let's meet at ten.

2.17

Good evening, I'm Angela Jones, and here is the weather forecast for tomorrow, March 21st. Well, it's going to be a cold day in the north-west with temperatures around two degrees Celsius. In the north-east it's going to snow in the afternoon. Rain is going to move into Wales in the morning, and it's going to rain in the south-west of England in the afternoon. It's going to be a cloudy day in the south of England. In the south-east it's going to be a lovely, sunny day. It's going to be windy in the Midlands, and in the east it's going to thunder. Well, that's all from me, have a nice day!

2.18

First conversation
A What are you doing tomorrow?
B Nothing, really. Why?
A It's going to be a lovely day.
B Great! Let's go for a walk in the country.

2.19

Second conversation
C Hello, Mam. I'm having an awful day. It's raining here and the children can't play outside.
D Oh, dear. Is it going to rain tomorrow?
C Yeah, but it's OK, They're at school tomorrow.

2.20

Third conversation
E Brrr. It's really cold today.
F Yeah. And it's going to snow tomorrow.
E That's March 21st! It's the first day of Spring!
F I think it's global warming!

2.21

Fourth conversation
G What's the weather forecast for tomorrow?
H Well, they say it's going to be windy.
G Very windy?
H Oh, yes. Very windy.

2.22

Fifth conversation
I Alright?
J Yeah.
I What are you doing tomorrow?
J I'm playing golf.
I Well, be careful. It's going to thunder in the afternoon. Don't stand under any trees.

2.27

Chris Now, the next question is for two thousand. Are you ready, Pat?
Pat Yes, Chris.
Chris The first modern Olympic Games were in 1896. Where were they? A, Paris? B, Athens? Or C, London?
Pat Um, well, the ancient Olympic Games were in Greece … so, I'm going to choose Athens.
Chris Sure?
Pat Yes, I'm sure, Chris. Athens.
Chris Athens is the right answer. You've got two thousand pounds, Pat! The next question is for four thousand. When was the first episode of 'Star Trek'? Was it A, 1966? B, 1976? Or C, 1996?
Pat Oh. Uh, it's a very old programme … mm, I think it was 1966 … I wasn't born then. Yeah, I'm sure it was 1966.
Chris 1966 is the … right answer, Pat! That's four thousand. Feeling confident?
Pat Not bad.
Chris Ready for the next question? This is for eight thousand. When were dinosaurs alive? Was it A, about 60 million years ago? B, about 6 million years ago? Or C, about 600,000 years ago?
Pat A, Sixty million years ago.
Chris That was quick! Are you sure?
Pat Yes, I'm sure, Chris. I'm a science teacher.
Chris And you've got eight thousand! Well done, Pat. Now for sixteen thousand … Who was Cleopatra? Was she A, The Queen of Rome? B, the Queen of England? Or C, The Queen of Egypt?
Pat C.
Chris C, The Queen of Egypt?
Pat Yes.
Chris That's your final answer?
Pat That's my final answer.
Chris You don't want to change it?
Pat No, Chris. C. The Queen of Egypt.

TRANSCRIPT

Chris And you've got sixteen thousand! Congratulations, Pat.
Pat Thank you.
Chris The next one's for thirty-two thousand. OK, Pat?
Pat Yes.
Chris Who was the author of 'Frankenstein'? Was it A, Agatha Christie? B, Mary Shelley? Or C, Charles Dickens?
Pat Oh. Um …
Chris Take your time, Pat.
Pat I've got no idea … it wasn't Charles Dickens. Um …was Mary Shelley a poet? Oh, I don't know … Agatha Christie. Um, yes, Agatha Christie.
Chris That's your final answer, Pat?
Pat Yes, Chris, I'm not sure, but … my final answer is Agatha Christie.
Chris Oh, I'm sorry, Pat! That's the wrong answer. The author of 'Frankenstein' was Mary Shelley, Oh, that's too bad, Pat. But you're going home with sixteen thousand. Give her a big hand!

2.29
The fifth of November, 1998.
The twenty-fourth of December, 1985.
The sixteenth of March, 2001.
The thirtieth of September, 2005.
The twenty-eighth of January, 1974.
The fifteenth of August, 2000.
The twelfth of May, 1999.
The twentieth of April, 1988.
The twenty-second of June, 2003.
The thirty-first of January, 2004.
The twenty-third of February, 2002.
The twenty-fourth of July, 1963.

2.31
R Excuse me, can I ask you some questions?
K Sure.
R What do you do?
K I'm a student at Harvard University.
R OK, what did you have for breakfast this morning?
K I didn't have an early class this morning, so I had breakfast in a diner. I had a hot breakfast. Eggs, potatoes, sausages, and pancakes.
R Did you have anything to drink?
K Yeah, an orange juice to start. Then coffee. Mmm, I guess I had two or three cups of coffee.

2.32
R Excuse me, can I ask you about breakfast?
A Sorry?
R It's a survey. About breakfasts. It only takes a minute or two.
A OK. What do you want to know?
R What did you have for breakfast this morning?
A Is that all?
R That's it.
A Oh, alright. I had a bowl of cereal and a banana.
R At home?
A Yes, at home.
R Anything to drink?
A Yes. I had a cup of tea. Are we finished?
R Yes. No more questions. Thank you.

2.33
R Excuse me, can I ask you some questions?
B What about?
R Breakfast. What did you have for breakfast this morning?
B This morning? Just a croissant.
R Did you have anything with it?
B Butter and jam. Do you need to know what kind of jam?
R No, I don't think so.
B It was strawberry.
R Right. Thank you. Um, did you have anything to drink?
B I had a pot of tea. Irish breakfast tea.
R That's fine. Oh, and where did you have breakfast?
B At the motorway services. I had an early start this morning. What about you? What did you have for breakfast?
R Me? Oh, no, I don't have breakfast!

2.37
Zoe Wow! Congratulations, Shaun. You were great!
Shaun Thank you, Zoe. I can't believe it.
Zoe So, Shaun, tell us about yourself. Where were you born?
Shaun Belfast, but my parents moved to Manchester later.
Zoe How old were you then?
Shaun I was ten.
Zoe When did you leave school?
Shaun Three years ago. When I was sixteen.
Zoe Where did you work?
Shaun In a supermarket.
Zoe When did you decide to be a singer?
Shaun I didn't. I wanted to be an actor. I studied acting in my free time. But I love singing.
Zoe Are you a fan of Eye Dolls?
Shaun Oh, yeah. This is the dream of a lifetime. They're all really great guys.
Zoe What's going to happen next?
Shaun We're recording a new album next week. Then we're going on tour.
Zoe Well, good luck with your new career,

TRANSCRIPT

Shaun.
Shaun Thanks, Zoe.

(2.45)
B I usually come here before work. I don't often come at weekends, but I do sometimes, if I'm not busy. I do about forty-five minutes or more. I did an hour yesterday, actually. But usually it's forty-five minutes.

(2.46)
E Well, I work here. I'm a trainer. I started at six forty-five this morning – we always open at seven. I usually have a coffee and something to eat at eight. I hardly ever sit down at other times.

(2.47)
A I come here three times a week. I didn't come yesterday. Twenty minutes a time. I never enjoy it! But it's good for you, that's what my doctor says. I always start on the exercise bike, then I jog for ten minutes, and I always lift some weights. I always have the same routine. Then I have a shower and I go to work.

(2.48)
F Gyms? Not me. You're joking. I go up and down this ladder all day, every day. And I always work with my arms. It's hard work too. I don't need a gym. I usually play football on Saturdays. That's my exercise for the week.

(2.49)
D I come once or twice a week, that's all. But I usually play tennis once a week, and I often swim on Saturdays. Why don't I walk downstairs to the changing room? That's funny. I always take the lift. It's a bit silly, really!

(2.50)
C I usually come here three or four times a week. I run every day too. I always do weight training. I don't often use the machines. Well, I sometimes do five minutes to warm up, that's all.

(2.52)
A OK, I'm thinking of a famous person.
B Right. Is the person male or female?
A You can only ask 'yes / no' questions.
B Sorry. Is the person male?
A No. That's your first question.
B So, she's female. Is she a politician?
A No, she isn't. Two.
B Is she an actor?
A Yes, she is.
B A female actor ... uh, is she British?
A No, she isn't.
B Is she American?
A Yes, she is.
B Is she African-American?
A No.
B OK. How many questions is that? And that wasn't a question!
A Six.
B Has she got dark hair?
A No, she hasn't.
B Has she got blonde hair?
A Usually, yes. Eight questions.
B Has she got blue eyes?
A Yes, she has.
B Is she beautiful?
A I think so. Yes. Ten.
B Was she in 'Lord of the Rings'?
A No, she wasn't. Eleven.
B Does she sing in her movies?
A I don't know. Maybe she does sometimes. But, she isn't famous for singing.
B Blonde, American ... is it Goldie Hawn?
A No, it isn't.
B Is she under fifty?
A Yes, she is.
B Under fifty ... is it Goldie Hawn's daughter? I can't remember her name ...
A No, it isn't. Fifteen.
B OK. Blonde American actor, beautiful, under fifty ... It's time to guess!
A If you want.
B Cate Blanchett?
A No. Sixteen.
B Er ... Julia Roberts?
A She isn't blonde. Seventeen.
B Has she got a Spanish name?
A Yes, she has. Eighteen.
B That's easy! Jennifer Lopez?
A No! Nineteen. And Jennifer Lopez sings. And she isn't blonde.
B Oh, yes, I forgot.
A One last question.
B OK, um ...
A Only one question left.
B Yes, OK! Um ...
A Well?
B Cameron Diaz?
A Oh, yes. That's right.

(2.55)
Mum Hello?
Alex Hi, Mum! It's me, Alex! I'm calling from California!
Mum What time is it there?
Alex It's ten o'clock on Wednesday evening.
Mum Well, it's six o'clock on Thursday morning here.
Alex Oh, sorry! I forgot!
Mum That's all right, dear. I'm awake now. Are

TRANSCRIPT

you having a good time?
Alex Oh yes, we're having a fantastic time.
Mum Where are you?
Alex We're in LA ... Los Angeles.
Mum Oh. Have you been to Universal Studios yet?
Alex Yes, we have. We went there on Monday.
Mum What was it like?
Alex It was great. The kids loved it.
Mum Oh. And have you been to Long Beach?
Alex Yes. We went there yesterday.
Mum Did you see the Queen Mary?
Alex Yes. And we've been to Disneyland.
Mum When did you go there?
Alex Today. We've just got back to the hotel. The kids are asleep. They're really tired.
Mum Have you been to Palm Springs yet?
Alex Not yet. We're going there tomorrow ... well, today British time!
Mum What about the National Park? Have you been there?
Alex You mean the Joshua Tree National Monument? We're going there on Friday. Then we're going to Sea World in San Diego on Saturday.
Mum When's your flight?
Alex Sunday. After lunch.
Mum Oh. How long does it take?
Alex Nearly twelve hours. So, see you on Monday.
Mum All right, dear. Have a nice time. Give my love to everyone. Bye.
Alex Bye.

(2.64)
Woman What are you playing?
Man Shh.
Woman What?
Man Road Race Four.
Woman Which is your car?
Man The red one. It's second – there's only one car in front. There it is ! OK. I'm going to pass it ... come on, come on ... I'm passing the blue car ... Yes! I'm in front ... I've passed it. I've won! Oh, no. Oh, how did that happen?
Woman Can I have a go now, then?

(2.65)
Man Oh, it's Debbie Toft – Inca Adventure. How far has she got?
Woman She's climbed the mountain. She's in the forest section now.
Man That's difficult. Has she been to the pyramid?
Woman No. Where is it?
Man It's on the other side of the river.
Woman Can she swim across?
Man No, the river's full of piranha fish.
Woman OK ... so ... She's going to jump.
Man Yes, but be quick ...
Woman Right ... she's jumping the river. And ... she's jumped across the river. What next?
Man The pyramid's along that path ...
Woman You mean, the path with the boa constrictor?
Man That's the one.
Computer Debbie Toft has lost three lives. That's the end of this adventure. Do you want to play again?

(2.66)
Man A OK. He's got the ball, and he's running towards the goal. He's gone round two defenders ... There's only the goalkeeper now. Is he going to score? Oh, no! It's gone over the bar. I don't believe it! He's missed!
Man B That was terrible – he's missed every time.
Man A Yeah. I'm losing seven-nil now.
Man B You need a new striker.
Man A I know.

(2.78)
1 I leave for the airport at seven thirty every morning. I work in the restaurant in Terminal Four.
2 They'll arrive at ten fifteen, I think. The scheduled time is ten thirty, but flights from the USA are often early.
3 We'll never get there on time. The traffic's bad today.
4 You'll finish soon. You've done most of the work. It'll only take you another five minutes.
5 They come home on Saturday. Here's their itinerary from the travel agency. Look: arrive Heathrow, Saturday 21st at 15.35.

(2.81)
Q Well, the score is ... our visitors from Batley University ten, and the Red Lion team eleven. Right, Red Lion, it's your turn. Are you ready?
RL man / woman Yes.
Q Right. Is the planet Venus bigger than the Earth, or smaller than the Earth?
RL Man I know this. It's bigger.
RL Woman Are you sure about that.
RL Man Yeah, I'm certain. Absolutely certain.
Q Sorry. That's the wrong answer. The Earth is bigger than Venus.
RL Woman You were so sure. I won't believe you next time.
Q So, Batley, your chance to catch up. Which is the highest mountain in the world?
BU man / woman Everest.
RL Woman That was too easy! Our question

was a lot more difficult.
Q There are some easy ones and some difficult ones. Yes, it's Mount Everest. So it's a draw. Batley eleven, Red Lion eleven. And Batley gets the next question. Which is the most dangerous insect in the world?
BU man Um, it's a spider. The Banana spider from South America.
BU woman Or is it the Black Widow spider?
BU man The Banana spider's more poisonous. I read it somewhere. It can kill six people.
Q So what's your final answer?
BU woman We'll choose the Banana spider. He's studying biology.
Q And that's the wrong answer. The mosquito's the most dangerous insect in the world. Malaria kills one and a half million people a year.
BU man That's not fair! I mean, one mosquito isn't very dangerous.
Q That's the answer on the card. Sorry. Red Lion, your question. Are dogs more popular than cats as pets in Britain?
RL Woman No.
RL Man Yes.
Q Can you decide? Yes or no?
RL Man Dogs are more popular than cats.
RL Woman I disagree! Anyway, I don't like dogs.
RL Man Yes, but it's not about you. It's about most people.
RL Woman Oh, all right. Dogs.
RL Man We think dogs are more popular than cats.
Q Oh! That's wrong. There are seven million pet dogs in Britain, but there are eight million pet cats. So it's still a draw, with both teams on eleven points. And there's one more question. This is for both teams. Hands up if you know the answer. I'll take the fastest answer. Here's the final question. Which is the oldest university in North America? Right, Batley! You were there first.
BU woman Harvard University in Cambridge, Massachusetts.
Q Certain?
BU woman Yes.
Q That's the wrong answer. What about you, Red Lion?
BU woman I don't know, but I'll make a guess. Is it Princeton?
Q That's wrong too! The answer is the University of Mexico. That's older than any university in the United States. So it's still eleven-eleven. We'll take a ten-minute break, and come back with more questions.

(2.91)
Salim So, how are you getting on at college, Hashim?
Hashim Oh, it's OK, Grandad. I have to do a lot of work, though. I have to write an essay every week.
Salim You call that work? You young people don't know anything about work.
Hashim It's all right for you, Grandad. You're retired. You don't have to get up early.
Salim Not any more. But I've worked hard all my life.
Hashim I know. You've told me before.
Salim And I'll tell you again! When I was your age, I had to leave my family and all my friends in Pakistan. That was in 1959. I had to come here to England. It wasn't easy. I couldn't speak a word of English. I had to work all day, and go to evening classes every night. I couldn't go out every evening, like you!
Hashim Yes, I know, Grandad, but ...
Salim I had to send money to my parents every month.
Hashim But things are different now, Grandad ...
Salim Different! They certainly are. Now the parents have to give money to the children! They all have to have CD players, and computers, and cars, and designer clothes ...
Hashim But everyone has those things nowadays ...
Salim Well, I didn't! And we were happier then, I can tell you. Your grandmother and I had to wait five years before we got married. We had to save our money for a home. We lived over the shop. Your father was born there. He worked hard and went to university. He didn't complain ...
Hashim Yeah, I know. Look, Grandad, I've got to go ...
Salim It's always the same. Young people never listen!

GRAMMAR

Reference: Talking about grammar

Letters and numbers

vowels	a, e, i, o, u, (y), my, fly, why?, by, cry
consonants	b, c, d, f, g, h, j, k, l, m, n, p, q, r, s, t, v, w, x, y, z
	y in young, yes, yellow, you, your
capital letters	A, B, C, D, E ...
double letters	pp, ll, tt, ss ...
numbers	one, seventeen, two hundred and thirty-eight
ordinal numbers	first, second, third, fourth, fifth, sixth, twenty-first

Determiners

indefinite articles	a, an
definite articles	the
demonstratives	this, that, these, those
possessive adjectives	my, your, his, her, its, our, their
adjectives	good, bad, red, large **comparative**: better, best
quantifiers	some, any, much, many, a lot, several ...

Nouns

nouns	apple, pen, computer, man, sandwich, pizza
proper nouns	Anna, David, Mrs Smith, France, Chicago, River Thames
singular nouns	book, watch, baby, woman, person
plural nouns	regular: books, watches, babies **irregular**: women, people
countable nouns	(There are some) apples, chairs, people ...
uncountable nouns	(There is some) water, petrol, money ...
gerunds	cooking, swimming, flying
genitive	Anna's, Charles's, The Beatles', The children's

Pronouns

subject pronoun	I, you, he, she, it, we, they
object pronoun	me, you, him, her, it, us, them
indefinite pronoun	anything, something, nothing, nowhere, anyone ...

GRAMMAR

Adverbs

time words	yesterday, now, tomorrow, last week, next year
adverbs of frequency	always, never, sometimes, usually
adverbs of manner	quickly, slowly, quietly **irregular**: well
introductory adverbs	Suddenly, Immediately, Luckily,

Other groups

linking words	and, but, or, so, because
prepositions of place	in, on, under, by
prepositions of movement	through, across, along, down
question words	Who? What? When? Where? How? Why?

Verbs

verb (lexical verb)	come, go, work, eat, drink
auxiliary verb	am, is, are, was, were, do, does, did, have, would
modal verb	can, can't, will, won't, would, could, must
contraction	I'm, I'd, I've, he's, I'll, What'll, don't, can't, hasn't, won't
past participle	been, seen, gone, born, done, eaten
infinitive	infinitive: to go, to be bare infinitive/base form: go, be
imperative	Listen. Don't talk. Be quiet. Come here.
positive	I'm listening. I work in an office. I was there.
negative	I'm not listening. I don't work in an office.
question	Are you listening? Do you know? Have you done it?
short answer	Yes, it is. Yes, I do. No, they aren't. No, he doesn't.
present simple	I live in London. He works in a bank. She doesn't know.
present continuous/progressive	She's wearing a hat. I'm looking for a DVD.
past simple	I went there. She didn't understand. Did you know?
present perfect	I've been to London. I haven't seen the Taj Mahal.
future simple	I'll do it tomorrow. Will you be there at six?
going to future	I'm going to do it. We aren't going to see them.
have to / had to	I have to go there. / I had to do it . / I didn't have to work.
regular	listen / listened / listened, walk / walked / walked
irregular	see / saw / seen, go / went / gone
tense	present, past, future
aspect	simple, continuous (also called progressive), perfect

GRAMMAR

Unit 1: *be* – singular

Positive and negative

I	'm	English.
	am	a student.
	'm not	from London.
	am not	
You	're	
	are	
	aren't	
	are not	
He	's	
She	is	
	isn't	
	is not	

Questions

Am	I	a student?
		English?
		from London.
Are	you	
Is	he	
	she	
Is	he	

Short answers

Yes, you are.
No, you aren't.

Yes, I am.
No, I'm not.

Yes, he is.
Yes, she is.
No, he isn't.
No, she isn't.

Subject pronouns	I	you	he	she
Possessive adjectives	my	your	his	her

Unit 2: *be* – plural

Positive and negative

We	're	English.
You	are	students.
They	aren't	from London.
	are not	

Questions

Are	we	English?
	you	students?
	they	from London?

Short answer

Yes, we are.
No, we aren't.
Yes, they are.
No, you aren't.
No, they aren't.

Subject pronouns	we	you	they
Possessive adjectives	our	your	their

Unit 3: *a, an*

Remember that the sound of the next word is important, not the spelling.

a	before the sound of a consonant: b, c, d, f, g, h, j, k, l, m, n, p, q, r, s, t, v, w, x, y, z
an	before the sound of a vowel: a, e, i, o, u

y is a consonant at the start of a word, but is sometimes a vowel in the middle, or at the end of a word: m**y**, b**y**, cr**y**, wh**y**, happ**y**, sill**y**, bus**y**

Question words (units 1 to 3)

Where	are	you	from?
	is	she	
What	is	your	name?
		his	phone number?
How much	is	that?	
		an orange juice?	
How old	are	you?	
		your parents?	
	is	he?	
		she?	
How	are	you?	
		your parents?	
	is	he?	
		she?	

Unit 4: *be* for talking about things

It	's	a	tree.
This	is		watch.
That	isn't	an	orange.
	is not		umbrella.
They	're		trees.
These	are		watches.
Those	aren't		oranges.
	are not		umbrellas.

What	is	it?
	are	they?

This	book	is	new.
That	computer	isn't	old.
These	books	are	grey.
Those	computers	aren't	

Don't write the contraction **'s** after *this*.
Don't write the contraction **'re** after *these*, *those*.

*What's **this**? **It's** a dictionary. What are **these**? **They're** English books.*

Unit 5: *has/have got*

I	've	got	a	car.
You	have			
We	haven't		an	old car.
They	have not			
He	's		some	pens.
She	has		two	books.
	hasn't		ten	
	has not			

Have	you	got	a	car?	Yes, I have.
	we				No, you haven't.
	they		an	old car?	Yes, they have.
	I				No, we haven't.
Has	he		any	books?	Yes, she has.
	she			pens?	No, he hasn't.
	it		a	café?	Yes, it has.
			any	shops?	No, it hasn't.

Note: You see these forms in formal written English.
I have a book. He hasn't a sister. Have you a car? Has he any books?
You see this more in American English. *Do you have a car? I don't have any books.*

Unit 6: Present simple tense

Present simple: positive

I	work	in an office.
You		in a hotel.
We		from 9 to 5.
They		outside.
He	works	
She		

Present simple: negative

I	don't	work	in an office.
You	do not		in a hotel.
We			from 9 to 5.
They			outside.
He	doesn't		
She	does not		

Remember! The **s** ending with *he*, *she*, *it* is only on the positive form.

Present simple: questions

Do	I	work	in an office?
	you		in a hotel?
	we		
	they		
Does	he		
	she		

Short answers

| Yes, I do. |
| Yes, they do. |
| No, you don't. |
| No, we don't. |
| Yes, he does. |
| No, she doesn't. |

***Wh*- questions**

Where	do	you	work?
Which company	does	she	work for?
What	does	his company	make?

GRAMMAR

Unit 7: *there is / there are*

Positive

There	is	a	mall.
		an	airport.
	are	some	shops.
		three	cinemas.
		several	museums.

Negative

There	isn't	a	mall.
	is not	an	airport.
	aren't	any	shops.
	are not		cinemas.
			museums.

Questions

Is	there	a	mall?
		an	airport?
Are	there	any	shops?
			cinemas?

Short answers

Yes, there is.
No, there isn't.
Yes, there are.
No, there aren't.

How many ... ?

How many are there? How many shops are there?

Adjectives

Adjectives have only one form. They're the same with singular and plural, and with male and female. They come before the noun.
It's an old town.   They're old towns.
an old woman   an old man   old people

Unit 8: Present simple ('timetable' present simple)

What time	does	it	arrive?
When		the flight	leave?
		the train	get there?
	do	you	
		we	
		they	

It	leaves	at 5.30.
The bus	arrives	at 17.30.
The flight	gets in	at half past five.
I	leave	
We	arrive	
They	get in	

Questions:
Which platform does the train leave from?
How do you come to work?
How long does it take?

Present simple spelling

+ s	I arrive ... / She arrives..., We get ... / It gets ...
+ es	They go ... / He goes ..., You do ... / She does ...
after: -ch, -sh -s, -x, -z	We finish ... / He finishes ..., I watch ... / She watches ...
-y → -ies	We fly ... / It flies ..., They try ... / She tries ...

Unit 9: Imperatives

Stand	over there.
Go	
Look	
Be	quiet.
	careful.

Don't	look	there.
	stand	
	go	
	be	silly.
		stupid.

Object pronouns

Look at **me**. This is for **you**. It isn't for **her**, it's for **him**.
Look at **it**. Take a photo of **us**. Give it to **them**.

Prepositions

I	'm	in front of	them.
He	's	behind	us.
She		next to	you.
It		on the left of	her.
We	're	on the right of	him.
You			me.
They			it.

I	'm	in the back	row.
He	's	in the middle	
She		in the front	
It			
We	're	at the back.	
You		in the middle.	
They		at the front.	

Unit 10: *can/can't* for ability

I	can	swim.	
You	can't	ski.	
He	cannot	run.	
She		play	the piano.
We		speak	French.
They		ride	a bike.

Can	you	swim?
	he	run?
	she	ski?
	we	
	they	
	I	

Yes, I can.
Yes, we can.
No, he can't.
No, they can't.

Can is a modal verb. Rules about modal verbs:

1 Modals don't add *s* in the third person singular.
   She can swim. He can't swim. NOT *She cans swim.*

2 We use the infinitive without *to* after modals.
   I can swim. NOT *I can to swim.*

3 There is no infinitive form. *can* NOT *to can*

4 You can use modals for the present and for the future.
   I can do it today. / I can do it tomorrow.

5 Modal questions have short form answers.
   Yes, I can. / No, they can't. / Yes, we can. / No, she can't.

6 Modals have negative forms.
   I can't swim. I cannot swim. NOT *I don't can swim.*

7 Modals form questions without auxiliary verbs.
   Can you swim? NOT *Do you can swim?*

GRAMMAR

Unit 11: Countable and uncountable nouns

Positive and negative

There	is	some	water.
	isn't	any	bread.
	are	some	apples.
	aren't	any	sandwiches.

Question

Is	there	any	water?
			bread?
Are			apples?
			sandwiches?

Short answers

Yes, there is.
No, there isn't.
Yes, there are.
No, there aren't.

Whose ... ? / Possessive 's

Whose	book	is	it?
	wine		
	books	are	they?

It	's	Jack's	book.
		Chloe's	wine.
They	're	James's	books.

Names ending with 's: Charles**'s** pen (OR Charles**'** pen)
Plurals: The children**'s** mother, The Beatle**s'** first record, the girl**s'** school, Jack and Chloe**'s** mother (NOT Jack**'s** and Chloe**'s**)

- *water* is uncountable but *glasses of water, litres of water, bottles of water* are countable.
- *money* is uncountable but *dollars, euros, cents* are countable.
- *time* is uncountable but *minutes, seconds, days, hours, years* are countable.
- Some words are difficult: *rice* is uncountable, but *peas* are countable.

Unit 12: *would like*

I	'd	like	some	milk.
You	would			of that.
He				
She			a	biscuit.
We			one	spoonful.
They			some	biscuits.
			two	of those.

Would	you	like	some	milk?
	he			of this?
	she			
	they		a	biscuit?
			some	biscuits?

Yes, please.
Yes, I would.
No, thank you. / No, thanks.
No, he / she wouldn't.

GRAMMAR

Which ... ?

| Which | book
one
ones | would | you
she
he | like? |

| I
You
He
She
We
They | 'd
would | like | the | blue
new
small
gold | one.
ones. |

Questions and offers

Use *any* with questions.
*Have you got **any** milk?* is a question.
The answer is *Yes, I have* or *No, I haven't*.
*Would you like **some** milk?* is an offer.
The answer is *Yes, please* or *No, thanks*.

I'd like ... / I want ...

The meaning is the same.
I'd like is more polite than *I want*.
Would you like ...? is more polite than *Do you want ...?*

> **Common mistake:** When you are offering something, say *Would you like (a drink)?* NOT *Do you like a drink?*

Unit 13: Present continuous formulas

I'm looking for (the station).
I'm trying to find (Bond Street).
No, thanks. I'm just looking.
Are you finding everything OK? (very frequent in shops in the USA)

can / may

Can I help you? = May I help you?
In these examples use *can* NOT *may*.
Sorry, I can't help you. / Can you help me?

Giving directions: formulas

It's not far. / Is it far? You can't miss it.
It's on the right / left. Turn right / left.
Go along (Oxford Street) / Go past (Selfridges).
You can walk / take a tube / take a bus / take a taxi.
It's at the (other) end.

GRAMMAR

Unit 14: Present continuous tense

Positive and negative

I	'm am 'm not am not	walking. going home. listening. working.
You	're are aren't are not	hiding. playing.
He She It	's is isn't is not	

Questions

Am	I	walking? going home? listening? working?
Are	you	hiding? playing?
Is	he she it	

Short answers

Yes, you are.
No, you aren't.

Yes, I am.
No, I'm not.

Yes, he is.
Yes, she is.
No, he isn't.
No, she isn't.

Wh- questions

What	are	you they we	doing? watching? looking for?
	is	he she it	
	am	I	

Use the present continuous for:

- things happening now.
  I can't speak to you now. I'm watching a TV programme.
- things happening over a long period of time.
  I'm reading 'Lord of The Rings' at the moment.
- describing.
  She's wearing a blue dress.
- future plans.
  I'm meeting her tomorrow evening at 7.30.

Spelling

+ *ing*	do → doing look → looking watch → watching
- *e*, + *ing*	hide → hiding live → living ride → riding
double the consonant	stop → stopping swim → swimming travel → travelling *

* *travel* → *traveling* in American English.

GRAMMAR

Unit 15: Likes and dislikes

I You We They	like don't like love hate	coffee. classical music. travelling by air. playing tennis. doing exercise. cooking. eating in restaurants. dogs.
He She	likes doesn't like loves hates	

These verbs are sometimes called **non-progressive** verbs because they usually appear in the present simple tense. Others examples are *know*, *understand*, *think*.
The present continuous tense is usually wrong with these verbs:
I like tea. NOT *I'm liking tea*.

We use a plural noun after these verbs:

*I **like dogs**.* NOT *I like dog*.
*I don't **like** rude **people**.* NOT *I don't like rude person*.

Verbs like *love*, *hate*, *like* are usually followed by an *–ing* form (or **gerund**).

False rule: Some older grammar books say *like* and *love* are **always** followed by an *–ing* form. This isn't always true. Some people say *I like **to play** tennis*, but it *is* true that *I **like playing** tennis* is more frequent. *I like **play** tennis* is always wrong.

so, really

Use *so* or *really* before adjectives:
*It's **so** nice.*
*You're **so** kind.*
*It's **really** nice.*

Use *really* before verbs:
*I **really** like it.*
*It **really** suits you.*

GRAMMAR

Unit 16: Present continuous tense for future arrangements

I	'm 'm not	meeting seeing	him her	tomorrow. next week.
You We They	're aren't		them you us	on the 21st. at 9.45. at lunchtime.
He She	's isn't		me Ann	

Going to future

(it) + *going to* + bare infinitive

It	's isn't	going to	rain. snow. thunder.

going to + be + adjective

It	's isn't	going to	be	hot / cold. sunny / cloudy. warm / cool.

going to + bare infinitive

What	are is	you she	going to	do?

I	'm 'm not	going to	stay at home. go shopping. buy a new car.
You We They	're aren't		
He She	's isn't		

going to go
- We can say: *I'm going home.* or *I'm going to go home.*
They are both correct. But people don't like repeating the verb, so *I'm going home* is more frequent.
- *going to* often sounds like *gonna*. You can see *gonna* in writing in rock song lyrics.

Unit 17: *be* – past simple tense

It isn't here now. It **was** here yesterday.
They aren't here now. They **were** here yesterday.

Positive and negative

I	was	there.
She	wasn't	here.
He		at home.
It		in London.
We	were	busy.
You	weren't	tired.
They		

Questions

Were	you	there?
	we	here?
	they	at home?
Was	he	in London?
	she	busy?
	I	

Short answers

Yes, (we) were.
No, (they) weren't.

Yes, (she) was.
No, (I) wasn't.

Where were you yesterday?
Who was there?

to be born

I	was	born	in	Ireland.
She	wasn't			hospital.
He			on	January 23rd.
We	were		at	2 a.m.
You	weren't			home.
They				

GRAMMAR

Unit 18: Past simple tense, irregular verbs

Positive

I / You / He / She	went	there / to Paris	yesterday. / last week. / last month.
	had	a holiday	last year.

Negative

I / You / He / She / We / They	didn't / did not	go	to Paris / there	yesterday. / last week. / last month.
		have	a holiday	last year.

Questions

Did	I / he / she	go	to Paris? / there?
	we / you / they	have	a holiday?

Short answers

Yes, I did. / No, I didn't.
Yes, he did. / No, he didn't.
Yes, she did. / No, she didn't.
Yes, we did. / No, we didn't.
Yes, you did. / No, you didn't.
Yes, they did. / No, they didn't.

Wh- questions

What	did	you / he	do? / see?

- There are about 200 irregular verbs in English. Most are frequent verbs, like *had*, *went*, *came*, *did*.
- You need to learn the positive form (*went*) but you can make the question and negative from *did* + present (**Did** you **go**? / I **didn't go**.)

Unit 19: Past simple tense, regular verbs

Past simple: regular verbs

Positive

I / You / He / She / We / They	lived / worked / moved / travelled / studied	there	in the 1990s. / last month. / last year. / in 2004.

Negative

I / You / He / She / We / They	didn't / did not	live / work / move / travel / study	there	in the 1990s. / last month. / last year. / in 2004.

GRAMMAR

Questions

Did	I	live	in Paris?
	he	work	
	she	move	
	we	travel	
	you	study	
	they		

Short answers

Yes, I did. / No, I didn't.
Yes, he did. / No, he didn't.
Yes, she did. / No, she didn't.
Yes, we did. / No, we didn't.
Yes, you did. / No, you didn't.
Yes, they did. / No, they didn't.

***Wh-* questions**

Where	did	you	live?
		we	work?
		they	study?
		I	travel?
		he	move?
		she	
		it	

Spelling

+ ed	want → wanted need → needed work → worked
+ d	like → liked, love → loved, hate → hated live → lived
consonant + *y* to *–ied*	try → tried cry → cried worry → worried
double the consonant	stop → stopped program → programmed travel → travelled*

* In American English, they write *traveled* not *travelled*

- All 'new' verbs in English are regular:
  video → *videoed   text someone* → *texted someone   key* → *keyed*
- Scientific and technical verbs are regular.
- Some verbs have regular **and** irregular forms: *learn**ed** / learn**t**, burn**ed**/ burn**t**, spell**ed** / spel**t**, dream**ed** / dream**t**.* The regular form is becoming more common.
- When you note regular verbs, note the pronunciation of the ending: [t], [d], [ɪd]

Unit 20: Prepositions

Prepositions of movement are in a group with **prepositions of place**.
In *He's coming **down** the stairs*, **down** is a preposition.
In *He's sitting **down**,* **down** is called an adverb in some grammar books.
Don't worry about the difference.

Introductory adverbs
These begin a sentence:
Finally … Suddenly … Luckily …

Unit 21: Adverbs of frequency

Adverbs of frequency come before the present simple tense

I / You / We / They	always / usually / often / sometimes / hardly ever / never	wake up / get up / have breakfast / leave home	at 7 o'clock. / at 6.30. / early.
He / She		wakes up / gets up / has breakfast / leaves home	

Adverbs of frequency come after the verb *be*

I	'm / am / was	always / usually / often / sometimes / hardly ever / never	late. / busy. / tired. / here.
You / We / They	're / are / were		
He / She	's / is / was		

How often do you do these things?

I / You / We / They	come here / have lessons	once / twice / three times / four times	a week. / a day.
He / She	comes here / has lessons	everyday.	

How often	do	you / they	see / meet	her? / him? / them? / us?
	does	he / she		

Unit 22: comparison of present continuous/simple

Uses of the present continuous tense:
1. **now** *He's cooking dinner at the moment.*
2. **over a long period of time** *I'm saving money for a new car.*
3. **describing** *He's wearing jeans.*
4. **future plans** *I'm meeting him on Monday at 12.30.*

Uses of the present simple tense:
1. **general** *I work in a bank. I live in Boston.*
2. **routines** *I get up at 7.30.*
3. **with frequency adverbs** *I usually drink tea with meals.*
4. **some verbs are usually present simple** *like, love, hate, know, understand, mean*
5. **timetables** *The plane leaves at 7.30. The bus arrives at 4.56.*
6. **truths, facts** *Water freezes at 0°C. The sun rises in the east.*

Unit 23: Present perfect simple tense

Positive and negative

		been	to	Spain.
I	've			Portugal.
You	have			Madrid.
We	haven't			Lisbon.
They	have not			the bank.
He	's			a circus.
She	has			a rock concert.
It	hasn't			
	has not			

Questions

Have	you	ever	been	to	Paris?
	they				a circus?
	we				
	I				
Has	he				
	she				
	it				

Yes, I have. / No, I haven't.
Yes, they have. / No, they haven't.
Yes, we have. / No, we haven't.
Yes, you have. / No, you haven't.
Yes, he has. / No, he hasn't.
Yes, she has. / No, she hasn't.
Yes, it has. / No, it hasn't.

Negatives with *never*

*I've **never** been there.   She's **never** been to France.*

Past participles: *been / seen*

Present	Past	Past participle
am / is / are	was / were	been
see / sees	saw	seen

*Have you ever **been** to London? Yes, I have.*
*Have you ever **seen** Prince William? Yes, I have.* (but we don't know **when**)

Use the past simple to talk about **when** things happened.
*When **did** you **go**? (I **went** to London) last year.*
*When **did** you **see** (him)? He **visited** my city five years ago.*

ago

two	seconds	ago.
five	minutes	
ten	hours	
fifteen	days	
	weeks	
	months	
	years	

GRAMMAR

Unit 24: Comparison of present perfect / past simple

Present perfect simple tense
We think about the past and the present at the same time:

Past: I saw the film last week. **+** **Present connection:** So, now I know the story of the film.

Yes, I've seen the film. It's terrible.

Past simple tense
We think about the past, not the present.

Past: I went to school in London. **Present:** But there's no connection with the present. I left years ago.

I went to school in London.

Finished action		Present perfect		Present connection
I found €20 in the street 2 minutes ago.	→	Look! I've found €20!	←	I've got it in my hand now. I'm showing it to you now.
I did my homework last night.	→	Yes, I've done my homework.	←	The teacher is asking me about the homework now.
He went to Spain yesterday.	→	He's gone to Spain.	←	He's in Spain now. He isn't here.

Regular verbs
The past participle is the same as the past simple:
I **passed** an exam last year. I've just **passed** another exam (this year).

Irregular verbs:
Sometimes the past participle is different from the past simple:
go → went → gone   fly → flew → flown
Sometimes the past participle is the same as the past simple:
buy → bought → bought   have → had → had
When you learn new verbs, try to note all three forms:
do → did → done

Past participles: irregular verbs

Present	Past	Past participle
am / is / are	was / were	been
buy / buys	bought	bought
do / does	did	done
eat / eats	ate	eaten
find / finds	found	found
fly / flies	flew	flown
go / goes	went	gone
meet / meets	met	met
win / wins	won	won

GRAMMAR

Past participles: regular verbs

Present	Past	Past participle
jump	jumped	jumped
arrive	arrived	arrived
want	wanted	wanted
study	studied	studied
travel	travelled	travelled

been / gone

- been is the past participle of the verb **be**:
  *Have you ever **been** on TV? Yes, I have. I **was** on TV three years ago.*
  BUT we sometimes use **been** like a past participle of **go**:
  *Have you ever **been** to Portugal? Yes, I have. I **went** there last year.*

- gone is the past participle of **go**:
  *Is Mrs Smith here? No, she isn't. She's **gone** to the bank.*
  been = here now. **gone** = not here now.

- There are some small differences between British and American English. For example:
  UK: *get / got / got* **US:** *get / got / gotten*
  UK: *dive / dived / dived* **US:** *dive / dove / dove*

Unit 25: *will / won't*

Positive and negative

I / You / He / She / We / They	'll / will / won't / will not	do it. / help. / be there.

Questions

Will	you / he / she / we / they	help? / do it? / be there?

Short answers

Yes, I will. / No, I won't.
Yes, he will. / No, he won't.
Yes, she will. / No, she won't.
Yes, we will. / No, we won't.
Yes, they will. / No, they won't.

Requests: *Will you help me with my maths?*   *I'll have a coffee, please.*

Deciding: You decide either *I'll do it* or *I **won't** do it.* e.g. *I'll answer the phone ...*

Agreeing to do something / Promising: This is usually a positive reply to someone.
*OK, I'll do it. / Yes, I **will**.*

Refusing: This is a negative reply. *Sorry, I **won't** do that. / No, I **won't**.*

GRAMMAR

Unit 26: The future

It**'ll** happen.   She**'ll** be late for work.   I think I**'ll** go to London on Sunday.
It **won't** happen.   He **won't** be on time.   They **won't** be at the party.

Positive and negative

I	'll	do it	later.
You	will	be there	soon.
He	won't	see her	at 5 o'clock.
She	will not	go there	tomorrow.
We		meet him	next week.
They			on Saturday.

Questions

Will	you	do it	later?
	he	be there	soon?
	she	see her	tomorrow?
	we	go there	next week?
	they	meet him	on Saturday?
	I		

Wh- questions

Where	will	you	go?
When		he	
Why		she	
Who		we	see?
What		they	do?
How old		I	be?

Unit 27: Comparatives

	Adjective	Comparative	Superlative
short adjectives	young high	younger higher	the youngest the highest
short adjectives ending in -*e*	nice	nicer	the nicest
short adjectives ending in a vowel + one consonant	hot big wet	hotter bigger wetter	the hottest the biggest the wettest
short adjectives ending in a vowel + *w*	slow low	slower lower	the slowest the lowest
adjectives ending in -*y* long adjectives	happy popular important	happier more popular more important	the happiest the most popular the most important
irregular	good bad	better worse	the best the worst

GRAMMAR

- Superlatives can be facts or opinions:
  *The Pacific is the big**gest** ocean.*
  *He's the **best** player in the team.*
- We use superlatives when we compare something (or someone) with the group it is in, and place it first.
- We usually use *the* before superlatives.
- We often use *than* after comparatives.
- We use comparatives to compare something or someone with other things or people.
  *I'm **older than** my sisters.*
  *He's **better than** Owen or Beckham.*

> **False rules:** Some older grammar books tell you to use the comparative for two things and use the superlative for three or more things.
> This is a **false rule**. We can use comparatives for larger groups:
> *She's **younger than** the other three musicians.*
>
> We can use superlatives for two things or people.
> *I'm terrible at tennis. My sister's **the best** tennis player.*
> *My sister's the better tennis player* is correct, but sounds formal and old-fashioned.
> BUT we say *Maria's better than Anna*, because there is a comparison with someone else.

Unit 28: Comparison of adjectives / adverbs of manner

Adjectives tell us more about a noun.
*It's a **red** car.*
*She's a **better** player than me.*

Adverbs tell us more about a verb.
*He spoke **loudly**.*
*They drove **quickly**.*
Notice the word order.

	Adjective	Adverb
regular	loud	loudly
	slow	slowly
	quiet	quietly
	bad	badly
	nice	nicely
regular ending in *-y*	happy	happily
irregular	good	well

GRAMMAR

Unit 29: *could / couldn't*

Positive and negative

I	could	swim.	
You	couldn't		
He			
She		play	the piano.
We		speak	French.
They		ride	a bike.

Questions

Could	you	swim.
	he	
	she	
	we	
	they	
	I	

Short answers

Yes, I could.
Yes, we could.
No, he couldn't.
No, they couldn't.

could is a modal verb. It is the past of *can / can't*.

have to / had to: present

Positive

I	have to	get up early.
You		work.
We		
They		
He	has to	
She		

Negative

I	don't	have to	get up early.
You	do not		work.
We			
They			
He	doesn't		
She	does not		

Questions

Do	you	have to	get up early?
	they		work?
	we		
	I		
Does	he		
	she		

Short answers

Yes, I do.
Yes, they do.
No, you don't.
No, we don't.
Yes, he does.
No, she doesn't.

have to / had to: past

Positive

I	had to	get up early.
You		work.
We		
They		
He		
She		

Negative

I	didn't	have to	get up early.
You	did not		work.
We			
They			
He			
She			

Questions

Did	you	have to	get up early?
	they		work?
	we		
	I		
	he		
	she		

Short answers

Yes, I did.
Yes, they did.
Yes, he did.
No, she didn't.
No, you didn't.
No, we didn't.

Unit 30: *want to do / would like to do*

I You We They	want don't want 'd like would like wouldn't like	to	be	famous. rich.
He She	wants doesn't want 'd like would like wouldn't like			travel round the world. get a better job. meet famous people. lose weight.

In negative sentences *I don't want to ...* is more frequent than *I wouldn't like to ...* .

Purpose

so, because
He wanted to get some money, **so** he went to the cash machine.
He went to the cash machine **because** he wanted to get some money.

infinitive for purpose
He went **to get** some money.

present simple
*I often go there **to meet** my friends.*
*I come here **to study** English.*

past simple
*They went **to get** a drink.*
*We came **to study** English.*

present perfect
*He**'s gone** to get some money.*
*They**'ve gone** to get a drink.*
*We**'ve come** to study English.*

ACKNOWLEDGEMENTS

The Publisher and Authors would like to thank the many teachers and institutions who piloted this material in Brazil, China, Eire, France, Hungary, Italy, Mexico, Poland, Spain, and the UK.

Authors' acknowledgements:
In a complex series like this, which has taken several years to prepare, pilot and produce, many people are involved and have creative input. We wish to thank the many people at OUP who participated in making this book.
We would like to add our further personal thanks to Catherine Smith and Karen Jamieson (Project Managers and Student Book editing), Richard Morris (design for all components) and Sally Cooke (Teacher's Book, 3-in-1 Practice Pack).

Acknowledgements:
p. 70 Walkin' to New Orleans. Words and Music by Antoine 'Fats' Domino, Dave Bartholomew and Robert Guidry © 1960 EMI Catalogue Partnership, EMI Unart Catalog Inc. and EMI United Partnership Ltd, USA Worldwide print rights controlled by Warner Bros. Publications Inc/IMP Ltd Reproduced by permission of International Music Publications Ltd. All Rights Reserved: p. 105 Return to Sender by Otis Blackwell and Winfield Scott © 1962 by ELVIS PRESLEY MUSIC, INC. – All Rights Reserved – Lyric reproduced by kind permission of Carlin Music Corp., London NW1 8BD: p. 136 Leaving on a Jet Plane by John Denver © 1967 and 1972 Cherry Lane Music Inc. Assigned to Harmony Music Ltd., 11 Uxbridge Street, London W8 7TQ. Reproduced by permission of Bucks Music Group. All Rights Reserved.

Illustrations by:
Jamil Aquib pp. 151/2; David Aitchinson; pp. 38; Graham Berry pp. 62, 126, 183; Kate Charlesworth pp. 92, 128, 171; Stephen Conlin pp. 66; Johnty Clarke pp. 16, 78; Paul Dickinson pp. 154; Mark Duffin pp. 48, 60, 82, 125, 197, 206; Maureen and Gordon Gray p.12; Tim Kahane pp. 24 (icons), 68, 95, 127, 143, 164; Uldis Klavins p.72; Roger Penwill pp. 49, 84, 130, 184; Gavin Reece pp. 24, 65, 76, 86, 110, 194; Paul Sample pp. 123, 137, 192, 201; Mark Thomas pp. 50, 54/5, 131; Jonathan Williams pp. 14, 153

Commissioned photography by:
Gareth Boden pp. 8, 9, 10 (woman and man in gym), 11, 19, 20, 37, 44, 45, 56, 64, 69, 71, 80, 85, 100, 114,124, 134, 146, 149, 150, 162, 188, 193, 202, 205; Richard Morris: p. 107/8; Peter Viney pp. 17, 40/41, 47, 149/50, 157

The publisher would like to thank the following for their kind permission to reproduce copyright material:
Action Plus p. 52 (t) (Athol Gazard); AKG – Images p. 22 (bl) (Erich Lessing), p. 25 (l) (Wilhelm-Hack-Museum, Ludwigshafen), p. 88/89 (t) (Albert Meyer), p. 109 (Erich Lessing); Alamy p. 34 (Frank Chmura), p. 36 (Popperfoto), p. 52 (cl) (S Grandadam/ Robert Harding World Imagery/Robert Harding Picture Library Ltd), p. 183 (Peter Bowater), p. 186 (Colin Walton); Anthony Blake Photo Library p. 52 (cc) (Oceania); Associated Press p. 52 (br) (Phil Noble/ Pool); BAA Aviation Photo Library p. 43; BMW p. 27 (br); Bridgeman Art Library p. 23 (cr) (Private Collection); Corbis UK Ltd. p. 21(b) (Gianni Dagli Orti), p. 22/23 (Bettmann), 22 (c) (Archivo Iconografico, S.A.), p. 22 (t) (Christie's Images), p. 23 (cl) (Roger Wood), p. 23 (t) (EdimÈdia), p. 25 (r) (Burstein Collection), p. 35 (t) (Ted Horowitz), p. 42 (Neil Miller/Papilio), p. 44 (b) (Geoffrey Taunton/ Cordaiy Photo Library Ltd.), p. 52 (cr), p. 70 (Bettmann), p. 89 (tr) (Bettmann), p. 99 (cl) (Jennie Woodcock/Reflections Photolibrary), p. 99 (tl) (Walter Hodges), p. 117 (bl) (Galella Ron/Sygma), p. 117 (r) (Mitchell Gerber), p. 118 (cl) (Gary D. Landsman), p. 118 (cr) (Larry Lee Photography), p. 119 (br) (Michael Busselle), p. 120/121 (Robert Landau), p. 120 (b) (Tony Roberts), p. 120 (c) (Kim Kulish SABA), p. 120 (t) (Bill Ross), p. 121 (b) (Kevin Schafer), p. 121 (t) (Kelly-Mooney Photography), p. 133 (Richard Gross), p. 138/139 (Bettmann), p. 139 (r), p. 165 (Hulton-Deutsch Collection), p. 178 (Tim Graham); Courtesy of Apple p. 27 (l); Empics p. 138 (bcr); French Ministry of Culture and Communication p. 21 (t) (Regional Direction for Cultural Affairs – Rhone-Alpes Region – Regional Department of Archaeology); Getty Images pp. 99 (b) (Catherine Ledner/Stone), p. 99 (cr) (Brooklyn Productions/The Image Bank), p. 99 (tr) (Terry Vine/Stone); Hulton/Archive/Getty Images pp. 98, 176; Levi Strauss UK Ltd p. 27 (tr); Meteorological Office Library and Archive p. 185 (tl) (Crown Copyright); Nike UK Ltd p. 27 (tc); Oxford University Press/Hemera pp. 10 (cl), 10 (l), 18 (bl), 18 (br), 18 (cl), 18 (cr), 18 (tl), 18 (tr), 28 (l), 28 (r), 31 (b), 33 (cl), 33 (cr), 33 (l), 33 (r), 57 (cl), 58 (a), 58 (b), 58 (br), 58 (c), 58 (d), 58 (e), 58 (f), 58 (g), 58 (h), 58 (j), 58 (k), 58 (m), 58 (n), 58 (o), 58 (p), 58 (q), 58 (r), 58 (s), 58 (t), 58 (u), 58 (v), 58 (w), 58 (x), 58 (y), 58 (z), 79 (a), 79 (b), 79 (c), 79 (d), 79 (e), 79 (f), 79 (g), 79 (h), 79 (i), 79 (j), 79 (k), 79 (l), 91 (a), 91 (b), 91 (c), 91 (d), 91 (e), 91 (f), 91 (g), 91 (h), 101, 146 (c), 146 (l), 146 (r), 160, 168, 169 (l), 169 (r), 170 (a), 170 (b), 170 (c), 170 (d), 170 (e), 170 (f), 170 (g), 170 (h), 181 (l), 181 (r), 182, 185 (b), 189, 190 (a), 190 (b), 190 (c), 190 (d), 190 (e), 190 (f), 190 (g), 190 (h), 190 (i), 190 (j), 190 (k), 190 (l), 190 (m), 199 (a), 199 (b), 199 (c), 199 (d), 199 (e), 199 (f), 199 (g), 199 (h), 199 (i), 199 (j), 199 (k), 199 (l), 199 (m); Oxford University Press/Stockbyte pp. 32 (b), 32 (t), 57 (cr), 57 (l), 57 (r); Oxford University Press pp. 35 (b), 81 (Digital Vision), 96, 97, 118/9, 135, 136; Photo Scala, Florence p. 23 (br) (Museum of Modern Art, New York, United States); Press Association p. 90 (l); Raleigh Cycles p. 27 (cr); Rex Features pp. 29, 52 (bl) (David Hartley), 88 (c) (SNAP), 90 (r) (Munawar Hosain), 103 (b) (Peter Lawson), 103 (t) (Peter Lawson), 116 (bl), 116 (br) (SNAP), 118 (b) (Nicholas Bailey), 119 (t) (Hayley Madden), 185 (tc) (Ken McKay), 185 (tr) (Ron Sachs); Ronald Grant Archive pp. 31 (t), 88/89 (b), 116/117, 116 (tl) (Gaumont), 117 (cl) (20th Century Fox), 132, 138 (tc), 138 (tl) 140/141, 140 (l), 141 (r), 195 (b); Sony Ericsson UK & Ireland p. 27 (bc); The Field Museum, p. 42 (c) p. 89 (br) (John Weinstein); W & B Lack Photography p. 104